This book is due for return not later than the
last date stamped below, unless recalled sooner.

Waystage 1990

Council of Europe
Conseil de l'Europe

J. A. van Ek and J. L. M. Trim

PUBLISHED BY THE PRESS SYNDICATE OF THE UNIVERSITY OF CAMBRIDGE
The Pitt Building, Trumpington Street, Cambridge CB2 1RP, United Kingdom

CAMBRIDGE UNIVERSITY PRESS
The Edinburgh Building, Cambridge CB2 2RU, United Kingdom
40 West 20th Street, New York, NY 10011–4211, USA
10 Stamford Road, Oakleigh, Melbourne 3166, Austrailia

First published as *Waystage 1990* by J.A. van Ek and J.L.M. Trim
© Council of Europe 1991

This revised and corrected edition first published 1998
© Council of Europe

Printed in the United Kingdom at the University Press, Cambridge

A catalogue record for this book is available from the British Library

Library of Congress Cataloguing in Publication data applied for

ISBN 0 521 56707 6 paperback

Contents

Preface

Waystage 1990 is the latest, thoroughly revised, extended, corrected and reset version of *Waystage: an intermediary objective below Threshold Level in a European unit/credit system of modern language learning by adults* by J. A. van Ek and L. G. Alexander, in association with M. A. Fitzpatrick. This work was first published by the Council of Europe in 1977 and republished in 1980 by Pergamon Press for and on behalf of the Council of Europe under the title *Waystage English*.

Waystage was originally conceived in the context of the preparation for the broadcast-led Anglo-German multimedia co-production *Follow Me*. Overall, *Follow Me* was originally planned as a two-year English language course for use by the DVV (*Deutscher Volkshochschulverband*) in its adult education classes. The final objective was set as *The Threshold Level*, first produced for the Council of Europe by Dr J. A. van Ek, which sets down in specific detail, exemplified for English, what a language user needs to do by means of language in order to 'communicate socially with people from other countries, exchanging information and opinion on everyday matters in a relatively straightforward way, and to conduct the necessary business of everyday living when abroad with a reasonable degree of independence' (preface to *Threshold*, CUP 1998). An experiment conducted in Vienna *Volkshochschulen* showed that the full attainment of this objective under the normal conditions of adult education would take a full two years. Yet, realistically, it was likely that local conditions would oblige broadcasting and education authorities in many countries to use only the first year of the course. Together with the *Follow Me* course designers, van Ek therefore examined carefully the content of *The Threshold Level* and extracted what were considered to be the most basic categories within each of its parameters – the most essential situations, topics and functions, inescapable general notions and their simplest and most basic lexical and grammatical exponents to enable the learners to cope at least minimally in those communicative situations which may be most directly relevant to them. This specification then provided the basis for the first year *Follow Me* course design drawn up for the Council of Europe by L. G. Alexander. At first *Waystage* was not considered a legitimate terminal objective in its own right, but rather as one of many possible intermediate objectives on the way to threshold level. However, by 1980, experience with *Waystage* had shown that whilst 'we should not favour a "minimalism" which saw this first objective as a terminal goal for the mass of learners, it has in fact a coherence and breadth which make it a worthwhile objective in its own right'. (*Waystage English* p. viii) Learners who for one reason or another have only a strictly limited amount of time available for learning English will find its 'cost-effectiveness' very high.

In broadcasting terms, *Follow Me* was highly successful. First broadcast in 1979 to Germany, Austria and Switzerland, it has now been shown in some 70 countries to a combined audience of several hundred million learners. The success of this venture in international co-planning and co-production (notoriously difficult to achieve) was due, on the one hand, to the high professional expertise of the many partners involved in the planning, production, distribution and use of TV, radio and printed components, and on the other to what proved to be the universal relevance to language learners of the functional/notional framework set out in *Waystage*. However, no media product has an unlimited life. By 1989, it was time to plan for a replacement series, which BBC English again wished to situate in an international context under Council of Europe auspices. Meanwhile, a considerable amount of work had taken place within successive Council of Europe Modern Languages Projects towards the development of an enriched model for the specification of language teaching objectives, resulting in the publication in 1986–7 of J. A. van Ek's two-volume study on *Objectives for Foreign Language Learning*. The revision of the original threshold level specification as applied to English, 'to take account of developments in the fifteen years since it was conceived as a first pioneering experiment' was included among the priority areas and themes for the Council for Cultural Co-operation programme *Language Learning for European Citizenship* initiated in 1989. BBC English expressed their willingness to support revision of *The Threshold Level* and also of *Waystage*, which would follow similar lines. A similar willingness was expressed by the University of Cambridge Local Examinations Syndicate in view of the relevance of this revision to their continuing programme of examination reform and by the British Council in the light of its more general concern for curriculum development in the teaching of English as a foreign language. A thorough revision was accordingly undertaken and carried out in 1989–90 and published by the Council of Europe in 1991. That version forms the basis for the present publication, which has been further revised, corrected and reset.

The authors wish to acknowledge here with gratitude the support received from BBC English, UCLES, the British Council and the Council of Europe. We also wish to acknowledge our continuing indebtedness to L. G. Alexander and M. A. Fitzpatrick for the skill and judgement they brought to the fundamental task of honing down the original *Threshold Level* specification to produce the compact yet comprehensive *Waystage*. The results of that work are still apparent in the selection of functional and notional categories for *Waystage*.

Furthermore, van Ek's words in his introduction to *Objectives for Foreign Language Learning* are as relevant to *Waystage* as to *Threshold Level*: it is 'one of the results of many years of intensive collaboration and genuine interaction with colleagues from several European countries brought together in the framework of successive modern language projects of the Council of Europe. The number of those who in some way or other, directly or indirectly, have contributed to our study is so large that we can only say to them collectively. "Thank you all".'

J. A. van Ek

J. L. M. Trim

Introduction

1 Target population and relation to *Threshold 1990*

Waystage 1990 is an early learning objective designed for those who are interested in acquiring a general basic ability in English but who are unable or unwilling to commit themselves from the outset to an expenditure of time and energy that would take them to the level of competence described in a separate publication called *Threshold 1990*.

Any learning objective is necessarily based on considerations of *desirability* and *feasibility*, the latter aspect providing the limits of the extent to which the former can be realised. What is, in our view, desirable for learners to be able to do in and with the foreign language, so as to be in a position to achieve the full mobility that a command of English may provide, is described by us in *Threshold 1990*. It has to be recognised, however, that for many beginning learners – and particularly for those with (only) little educational experience – the feasibility of mastering the learning load represented by that objective may seem to be very doubtful indeed. At the same time it cannot be denied that the achievement of a lower level of ability than threshold level might be of considerable value to them. Rather than deterring these potential learners by asking them to set their sights higher than they would consider to be reasonable, we would propose to them a reduced learning load of a weight which past experience has indicated to be generally acceptable and also manageable within a comparatively short time. *Waystage 1990*, then, is the result of our attempt to derive from *Threshold 1990* a less demanding objective based on the same model and containing the same components. In spite of heavy reduction this objective should go a long way towards enabling the learners to satisfy their most urgent communication needs. The learning load involved is estimated to be about half of that required by *Threshold 1990*, which means that we think that, with proper guidance, the average learner should be able to master it in some 180–200 learning hours, including independent work.

The original *Waystage*, first published by the Council of Europe in 1977, was primarily designed as a halfway level, a point of articulation for courses leading up to threshold level. That it might also be a worthwhile objective in its own right was only a secondary consideration.

Meanwhile it has become clear that for many learners the achievement of a level at this height is a thoroughly satisfying experience and that, in fact, a large number of them may not feel the need to go much beyond this in the same language. We have taken this into account in designing *Waystage 1990*. It is now primarily meant as a worthwhile objective in its own right and secondarily as an intermediate objective on the way towards threshold level. It remains a rigorous selection from *Threshold Level*, in this case *Threshold 1990*, but the consideration of immediate usefulness and widest possible scope has been paramount in this selection. Nevertheless, as the name indicates, it has also been conceived as a station on the way to *Threshold 1990*. In fact, containing all the components that also constitute the higher level, it will allow the smoothest possible transition to further learning for *Threshold 1990*. There can be no doubt that this transition will be made by many learners. We expect that the successful completion of a *Waystage* programme will be a strong incentive for the undertaking of the further learning effort required in order to reach the higher objective, and we also expect that this will be true for many learners who, at first, had no intention to do so.

2 Economy

What, at *Waystage*, the learners are supposed to be able to do in the foreign language is described in general terms in Chapter 1 of this document. The rest of it contains the specification of this ability. This specification will make it clear that, in spite of the modest height of *Waystage 1990*, the linguistic and other resources that the learners have at their disposal at this level will, in fact, give them a fairly wide range of action in the foreign language. This is largely due to the economy that has been practised in the selection of the learning content. This has invariably been chosen with a view to giving the widest communicative range with the simplest means. One consequence of the application of this criterion has been the inclusion of a fairly comprehensive grammatical apparatus. It is a characteristic of grammar that with a limited number of elements it provides the means for large numbers of combinations and variations. The acquisition of a grammatical system, even if at this level this can only be a restricted system, is, consequently, to be regarded as a highly productive – and economical – activity.

3 Flexibility and adaptability

Waystage 1990 has been designed for the largest single target group that may be identified, that of general beginners. A single objective for a target group of this size can only serve its purpose if it is highly flexible and adaptable to a variety of needs and interests. At the same time it should be recognised that, in spite of all the variety that may be expected, all members of the target group will have quite a lot in common. For one thing, they all want to acquire a general ability in the use of English. This means that they will all have to be able to ask questions and to provide information, to elicit opinions, views, preferences, and to express them, to refer to past, present and future events, to express reasons why and conditions under which something may come to pass and to understand others doing so, etc. Also, they will have to be familiar with certain social conventions and common assumptions inherent in manners of expression in the English language, and they will need to be aware of how cultural differences may be reflected in communicative behaviour. And then, of course, they will also need experience in coping with the inevitable occurrence of situations which overtax their resources. All these elements of communicative ability – and many more – are included in *Waystage 1990*. Collectively, they constitute the general basic ability which we have attempted to describe and specify in this objective. In this respect, then, *Waystage 1990* is an appropriate objective for anyone who wants to learn English for purposes of communication, whatever their special interests may be. However, it has a further potential. Through its comprehensive system of categorisation and the open-endedness of the various specifications it offers virtually unlimited possibilities for such expansions as may serve the purposes of particular sub-groups of the target population. Not only may the various categories be separately expanded, but several of them contain slots for the insertion of further (sets of) elements. Thus, for instance, if we would consider the sub-group of those who would wish to learn English particularly for professional purposes, text types of a professional nature may be added to the reading component, the writing component may be expanded as required – for example, with certain types of standard letters – the topic specification may be supplemented with further topics of professional interest, and open-ended lists within the topics can be filled in accordance with the needs and interests of particular learner groups.

The adaptability of *Waystage 1990* is a consequence of its open-endedness and of its internal flexibility. This flexibility in itself may be exploited in a variety of ways and with different emphases in accordance with the educational context in which the learning of the foreign language takes place and the effects that this learning is meant to produce. For the learning of a foreign language is an educational experience which may benefit the learners in several different ways. If undertaken as part of an overall educational programme, foreign language learning may, through the contacts it provides with another culture, play an essential role in widening the learners' horizon, in stimulating their awareness of the potential validity of different value systems, of different ways of organising, categorising and expressing experience, etc. If viewed in the perspective of permanent education, a foreign language course may equip the learners with skills and insight that will facilitate the subsequent expansion of their ability in the foreign language concerned or the subsequent learning of one or more other foreign languages. If pursued in a social context, foreign language learning may contribute to the development of the learners' understanding of the complexities of personal interaction, and it may prepare them to function more effectively in social contacts, not only in the foreign language but also in their native language, etc.

Many more of the potential benefits of foreign language learning are listed in Van Ek, *Objectives for Foreign Language Learning, Vol. 1: Scope*, Strasbourg 1986. Which of these learning effects, and how many of them, are explicitly or implicitly aimed at in a foreign language course, depends on the educational context in which the course is offered and/or taken, as well as on the educational views of those who provide the course and/or of those who take it.

4 What is new in *Waystage 1990*?

Waystage 1990 is designed to fit into a wide variety of educational contexts and to suit a wide variety of learning aims. In this respect it corresponds not only to *Threshold 1990*, but also to its predecessor, the 1977 *Waystage*. The main difference is that now those components of communicative ability which particularly allow it to be related to a wider educational context are identified and explicitly incorporated into the objective. Thus, *Waystage 1990* includes discourse strategies, a sociocultural component, compensation strategies, and a 'learning-to-learn' component. In addition, it contains numerous major and minor improvements in the specification of those categories which were already distinguished in the original *Waystage* as well as certain adjustments reflecting differences in assumptions as to foreign language needs in the 1990s as compared to the 1970s.

Some of the improvements have been designed to make the specification more accessible. They include a redesigned grammatical inventory and the provision of a subject index. Other changes are of a more fundamental nature, such as the more liberal inclusion of items for 'understanding' only, the explicit treatment of selected intonation patterns, the addition of two new categories of language functions – 'structuring discourse' and 'communication repair', and the introduction of several open-ended items in the list of specific notions.

Such changes and additions as distinguish *Waystage 1990* from its predecessor result from experiences gained in various applications of the original version and of the earlier *Threshold Level* as well as from the further development of insights into the nature of communicative ability and implications of all this for educational practice. Much of this we owe to the rich literature bearing on 'communicative language learning and teaching' that has been produced in the last fifteen years or so. As authors of a new threshold level version as well as of a new waystage version we are particularly indebted to all those who, since the original threshold level for English came out, have undertaken the development of parallel versions for other European languages and in each case contributed insights of their own.

5 Learning load

Waystage 1990 has more components than the old one and in some cases – particularly 'reading' and 'listening' – it requires more of the learners than its predecessor did. At first sight, then, it might seem to represent a heavier learning load. It is our assumption, however, that in practice this will not be the case. The new components are largely concerned with the acquisition of strategies and the development of insights and awareness. Their incorporation will have a qualitative rather than a quantitative effect. It does not substantially increase the number of learning items but it will affect the presentation and practice of these items. It will involve, for instance, the selection of texts not only for (pragma-) linguistic relevance but also for sociocultural relevance or for relevance with regard to 'coping strategies'. It will also mean that learning tasks will have to be made transparent enough for the learner to understand how the performance of these tasks may contribute to the achievement of his or her aims. The promotion of the development of various types of insight and awareness will require the introduction of teaching/learning procedures which are not yet commonly found in language courses. One such procedure is described in the recently developed 'Stage 3 level' brochure of the International Certificate Conference. It concerns the development of sociolinguistic awareness and appropriate strategies and consists of three steps:

- exposure to a variety of situations in which such features as participant roles, setting, communicative goal, etc., significantly influence the choice of language forms;

- stimulating awareness of this influence through observation, reflection, discussion;

- involving the learner in similar situations for active practice.[1]

The introduction of such a procedure into a language course, we assume, will make learning more effective rather than more demanding.

---

1 *Foreign Languages in Adult and Continuing Education; Specifications for Stage 3 Level of the International Certificate Conference Language Certificate System: English*, third draft, Deutscher Volkshochschulverband e.V., Bonn-Frankfurt 1987.

No more do higher demands with regard to 'reading' and 'listening' necessarily increase the actual overall learning load. On the contrary: it is increasingly recognised that frequent exposure to texts – or the intensive practice of 'receptive skills' – will contribute substantially to the efficient development of productive ability as well. In fact, what we propose in *Waystage 1990* is much more in agreement with current educational practice than the more modest requirements of the original version.

Our conclusion is that, in terms of the average number of learning hours that may be required, the learning load of *Waystage 1990* will correspond to that of the original version and that, as stated in section 1 of this introduction, a total of 180–200 hours would seem to be a reasonable estimate.

1 The objective: description

The learners will be able to use the foreign language for the following purposes:

I carrying out certain transactions:

1 making arrangements (planning, tickets, reservations, etc.) for:

- travel
- accommodation
- appointments
- leisure activities

2 making purchases

3 ordering food and drink

II giving and obtaining factual information:

1 personal information (e.g. about name, address, place of origin, date of birth, occupation)

2 non-personal information (e.g. about places and how to get there, about the time of day, about various facilities and services, about rules and regulations, about opening hours, about where and what to eat, etc.)

III establishing and maintaining social and professional contacts, particularly:

1 meeting people and, if strangers, making their acquaintance

2 extending invitations and reacting to being invited

3 proposing/arranging a course of action

4 exchanging information, views, feelings, wishes, concerning matters of common interest, particularly those relating to:

- personal life and circumstances
- living conditions and environment
- occupational activities and interests
- leisure activities and social life

The learners will be able to carry out the above communicative activities in contacts with:

- native speakers of the foreign language
- non-native speakers of the foreign language (using the foreign language as *lingua franca*)

Such contact may occur:

- in a country or region where the foreign language is the native language
- in the learner's own country
- in a country or region outside the learner's own country, where the foreign language is not the native language

The learners will primarily be able to function in contacts involving the oral use of the foreign language, mainly face-to-face contacts but also those requiring the use of the telephone or of public media. Secondarily, where appropriate, they will be able to understand the substance and/or relevant details of written texts and to express themselves in writing. Both the text types to be understood and those to be produced will be specified subsequently.

2 Components of the specification

The *Waystage* specification is not a closed syllabus, nor is the communicative ability described in it confined to a strictly limited number of specific situations. On the contrary: it is aimed at providing the learners with an overall basic skill in using the foreign language which, although it is primarily directed towards the requirements of selected situations, should give the learners a far wider range of action as well as a solid basis for further language learning. Thus, in spite of the limitations of its content, which are inherent in the concept of an 'early learning objective', *Waystage* does provide the learners with an ability to manipulate the language for their own purposes. This means, for instance, that at *Waystage* learners can fulfil a fairly wide range of essential language functions, although with very simple means, and that they can also express a large number of generally used concepts as well as understand others expressing them. Moreover, they will have at their disposal a fair number of communication strategies that will enable them to make the most of their as yet limited resources. Also, they will have been specifically prepared for functioning in those situations in which, on the whole, they are most likely to need the ability to use the foreign language, while having the potential to make at least a good attempt at coping with other situations as well.

It is in accordance with the above considerations that the *Waystage* specification consists largely of components and items relevant to general basic communicative ability, the requirements of specific selected situations being met by – mainly – concrete vocabulary items.

Waystage, while being a worthwhile objective in its own right, marks the conclusion of a first significant phase for learners on their way to *Threshold*, the objective that gives them a more general freedom of action in the foreign language. To a large extent, then, the specification of *Waystage* is a selection from that of *Threshold*. This selection is based on what, in view of the general description of the objective (see Chapter 1), the learners are likely to need most in order to satisfy their most urgent communication needs. As is the case in *Threshold*, *Waystage* offers lists of recommended 'exponents', i.e. of those language forms which are estimated to enable the learners to do all the things specified in a highly economical manner. This means that whenever feasible those language forms have been chosen which offer a wide functional range. If the learners' linguistic resources are to be narrowly limited – as they necessarily are at this stage – it is all the more important that those resources should be selected which provide the widest possible range of action.

The same criterion of economy cannot be applied to language produced by others than the learners themselves. We therefore include a much larger selection of language forms that the learners may find it very useful to be able to understand, even if they cannot and need not produce them themselves. These exponents are marked ® to distinguish them from exponents recommended for productive use.

At *Waystage* the learners should be able to fulfil a number of language functions and to handle a number of notions, both notions that are generally involved in the use of language ('General Notions') and notions required in dealing with specific situations and themes ('Specific Notions'). Our specification of *Waystage*, then, starts with lists of selected language functions, general notions and specific notions, together with their recommended exponents.

What may be expected of learners at *Waystage*, as far as conversational ability is concerned, is obvious from the whole of the specification. Requirements for reading, listening (as a one-sided process) and writing are scattered throughout the specification and often only implied by it. After the earlier 'lists' we therefore provide separate surveys of these requirements in a chapter on 'dealing with texts' and in a short one on 'writing'.

A separate chapter is devoted to 'sociocultural competence' or the ability to relate language use to the sociocultural background of communication partners. For this chapter, too, a selection is made from *Threshold 1990*.

The exponents of language functions are likely to occur in sequences. If these sequences exhibit certain regularities in the order of their elements we may refer to them as 'patterns'. A chapter on 'verbal exchange patterns' (Chapter 9) deals with a number of patterns which are likely to occur in situations of oral language use that may be particularly relevant to members of the target group.

No matter what level a foreign language learner has reached, there will always be situations that overtax the learner's resources as a user of the foreign language. The lower the level achieved, the more often such situations are likely to occur and the more urgently the learner will need the ability to use certain strategies that may enable him or her to cope with the requirements of these situations nevertheless. The availability to the learner, then, of 'compensation strategies' is at least as important at *Waystage* as it is at *Threshold*. The acquisition of such strategies by the learners should be promoted from a very early stage onwards in a language course. Which strategies are acquired by individual learners and the rate at which they are acquired may vary enormously from one learner to another.

The point is not so much which strategies learners have acquired and to what extent they have acquired them at a given moment but that they have acquired such strategies as will suit their own purposes and fit their own personality. Consequently, we see no reason for attempting to differentiate with regard to this component between requirements for *Waystage* and for *Threshold*, and the specification we present in Chapter 10 is identical with the corresponding one in *Threshold 1990*.

Similarly, the chapter on 'learning to learn' (Chapter 11) does not differ from the corresponding one in *Threshold 1990*. There is no reason why the objective for this aspect should not be pursued from the first lesson of a language course onwards, nor why it should be any different for *Waystage* learners than for *Threshold* learners.

The present specification – like that for *Threshold 1990* – will be followed by a brief note on 'degree of skill' and by appendices containing a survey of relevant intonation patterns, a grammatical inventory, a recommended core vocabulary and a subject index.

3 Language functions

Introduction

In the present specification the language functions – what people *do* by means of language – are listed in six broad categories:

1 imparting and seeking factual information

2 expressing and finding out attitudes

3 getting things done (suasion)

4 socialising

5 structuring discourse

6 communication repair

The second category is the most comprehensive and is subdivided as follows:

2.1–2.4   factual: agreement, etc.

2.5–2.6   factual: knowledge

2.7–2.15   factual: modality

2.16–2.20 volitional

2.21–2.29 emotional

2.30–2.35 moral

The lists of functions under each category heading are the result of a two-step process of selection. The first step produced the list in *Threshold 1990* and the second step the present specification. The principle of selection has been throughout that the functions selected should meet the most likely and urgent needs of the learners and together they should be manageable within the estimated average learning time stated for the objective (see section 5 of the Introduction). In many cases exponents – sometimes even all the exponents of a function – are followed by the symbol ® (i.e. 'for receptive use only'). This symbol is used to indicate that a particular exponent, though likely to be encountered in contact with native speakers, is felt to be of lower priority in the learners' productive repertoire.

Language functions may be fulfilled directly and indirectly. They are fulfilled directly if an exponent is used in its conventional meaning, i.e. in the meaning that would normally be assigned to it if it were used in isolation. *'You should go now'* fulfils the function of 'advising others to do something' directly, whereas *'It's getting late'* – in its conventional meaning fulfilling the function of 'reporting' – may serve the same purpose indirectly. The possibilities for the indirect fulfilment of language functions vary in accordance with the situational and the linguistic context of a communicative act.

This variation is such that a systematic description and selection on behalf of our objective is not possible. The exponents we propose, therefore, are on the whole those which may be considered to fulfil the functions concerned directly. This does not mean that the indirect fulfilment of language functions should be avoided in course materials designed for *Waystage*. On the contrary, an attempt to do so might lead to highly unnatural language use.

Language functions for *Waystage* with recommended exponents

1   Imparting and seeking factual information

1.1   identifying (defining)
(with pointing gesture) this (one), that (one), these, those
me, you, him, her, us, them
the, this, that, these, those,
(+N) + *be* + NP
'This is the ˌbedroom.
I, you, he, she, it, we, they + *be* + NP
'He is the ˌowner of the ·restaurant.

1.2   reporting (describing and narrating)
declarative sentences
The 'train has ˌleft.
NP + say, think + complement clause
He ·says the 'shop is ˌshut.

1.3   correcting
As 1.1 and 1.2, with contrastive stress
ˈThis is the ·bedroom.
The ·train 'has ·left.

(correcting a positive statement)
No (+ tag)
ᵛNo.
'No it ᵛisn't.
negative sentences
Va·letta 'isn't in ᵛItaly.
(correcting a negative statement)
Yes (+ tag)
ᵛYes.
'Yes you ᵛdid.

1.4   asking
a for confirmation
   interrogative sentences
   'Did you ˌsee him?
   declarative sentences with high-rising intonation
   You 'saw him? ®
   short questions
   ˌAre you? ®
b for information
   wh questions
   (time) ˌwhen?
   (place) ˌwhere?
   (manner) ˌhow?

(degree) how ˌfar/ˌmuch/
ˌlong/ˌhot/etc.?
(reason) ˌwhy?
c seeking identification
  wh questions
  (person) ˌwho?
  (possession) whose + NP?
  'Whose ˌwatch is ·this?
  (thing) ˌwhat?
  which + NP?
  'Which ˌsport do you ·play? **ⓡ**

1.5   **answering questions**
a for confirmation
  Yes, No (+ tag)
  ˌYes (he ˌis).
  ˌNo (he ˌisn't).
b for information
  declarative sentences
  ('Where did you ˌgo?)
  I ·went to ˌLondon.
  (time)
  adverb, prepositional
  phrase
  ˌyesterday. At 'ten o'ˌclock.
  (place)
  adverb, prepositional
  phrase
  ˌThere. 'On the ˌtable.
  (manner)
  adverb, prepositional
  phrase
  ˌFast. With a ˌspoon.
  (degree)
  adverb, prepositional
  phrase
  ('How ˌhot is it?) ˌVery.
  ('How ·much do you ˌlike it?)
  'Better than ˅water.
  (reason) (because +)
  declarative sentence
  ('Why did you ˌleave?)
  Because I was ˌtired.
c seeking identification –
  see 1.1

2   **Expressing and finding
      out attitudes**

Factual: agreement, etc.

2.1   **expressing agreement with a
      statement**
  I aˌgree.
  'That's ˌright. **ⓡ**
  (with a positive statement)
  ˋYes (+ tag).
  (She's ˋnice!) ˋYes, she ˋis!
  Of ˌcourse. **ⓡ**
  ˌCertainly. **ⓡ**
  (with a negative statement)
  ˌNo (+ tag)
  (He 'doesn't look ˌwell.)
  ˌNo, he ˌdoesn't.
  Of ˌcourse ·not. **ⓡ**
  'Certainly ˌnot. **ⓡ**

2.2   **expressing disagreement
      with a statement**
  That's 'not ˌright.
  I 'don't aˌgree. **ⓡ**
  (with a positive statement)
  ˌNo (+ tag).
  'Certainly ˌnot. **ⓡ**
  I 'don't ˅think so.
  (with a negative statement)
  Yes (+ tag).
  (They 'aren't ˌFrench)
  'Yes, they ˅are
  I think + positive statement
  I·think he 'will ·come.

2.3   **enquiring about agreement
      and disagreement**
  Do(n't) you think +
  complement clause?
  'Do you ·think it'll ˌrain?
  'Do(n't) you ˌthink so (ˌtoo)?
  'Do(n't) you aˌgree? **ⓡ**

2.4   **denying something**
  No (+ negative tag)
  (You ˌsaw him)
  ˌNo, I ˌdidn't.

negative sentences with not,
never, no (adjective),
nobody ®, nothing

Factual: knowledge

2.5   **stating whether one knows
or does not know something
or someone**
I (don't) know (+ NP).

2.6   **enquiring whether one
knows or does not know
something or someone**
Do(n't) you know (+ NP)?

Factual: modality

2.7   **expressing ability and
inability**
NP + can (not) …

2.8   **enquiring about ability and
inability**
Can (not) + NP …?

2.9   **expressing how (un)certain
one is of something**
a strong positive
   I'm sure (+ that clause). ®
   I'm certain (+ that clause). ®
b positive
   declarative sentence
   I know + that clause.
c intermediate
   I ˇthink so.
   I think + that clause.
   I supˇpose/beˇlieve so. ®
   I suppose/believe + that
   clause. ®
d weak
   NP + may … ®
   Perˇhaps. ®
   I'm not ˇsure (+ that
   clause). ®
   I ˎwonder. ®

e negative
   NP + cannot … ®
   I 'don't ˎthink so.
   I don't think + that clause.

2.10   **enquiring how (un)certain
others are of something**
'Are you (·quite) ˎsure? ®
Are you (quite) sure + that
clause? ®
'Do you ˎthink so? ®
Do you think + that clause? ®

2.11   **expressing one is (not)
obliged to do something**
I/We (don't) have to …

2.12   **enquiring whether one is
obliged to do something**
Do I/we have to …?

2.13   **giving permission**
You can …
You may …
Yes.
Of ˎcourse (you·may). ®
('That's)·all ˎright.

2.14   **seeking permission**
May I …?
Can I …?
Let me … ®
Do you mind + if clause? ®

2.15   **stating that permission is
withheld**
(Please) don't (…).
No.
NP + must not … ®

Volitional

2.16   **expressing want, desire**
I'd like … (e.g. a drink, to go
now).
I want … (e.g. a drink, to go
now) (please).
May I have + NP (please)?

2.17 enquiring about want, desire
Would you like … (e.g. a drink, to go now)?
Do you want … (e.g. a taxi, to walk)?
What about … (e.g. a drink, going out)? ®

2.18 expressing intention
NP + *be* going to …
NP + will/'ll … ®

2.19 enquiring about intention
Are you going to …?
Will you …? ®

2.20 expressing preference
I('d) prefer + NP.
I('d) like + NP.
I'd rather … (than …). ®
I'd rather not (…). ®

Emotional

2.21 expressing pleasure, liking
NP + *be* (very) nice.
NP + *be* (very) pleasant. ®
I like + NP (very much).
I love … (e.g. books). ®

2.22 expressing displeasure, dislike
NP + *be* not (very) nice.
NP + *be* not (very) pleasant. ®
I don't like + NP (very much).
I hate … (e.g. cabbage, swimming). ®

2.23 enquiring about pleasure, liking, displeasure, dislike
Do(n't) you like + NP?
Would you like … (e.g. to go now)? ®

2.24 expressing hope
I' hope ˌso.
I (do) hope + that clause. ®

2.25 expressing satisfaction
·This/·That is 'very ˌgood/ˌnice.

2.26 expressing dissatisfaction
I 'don't ˌlike this/that.

2.27 enquiring about satisfaction
'Do you ˌlike this/that?
'Is ·this ·all ˌright (·now)? ®

2.28 expressing disappointment
'What a ˌpity!
·That's a ('great) 'pity! ®

2.29 expressing gratitude
ˌThank you ('very ˌmuch).
That's 'very ˌkind of you. ®

Moral

2.30 apologising
I am ('very) ˌsorry!
ˇSorry!
I am 'so ˌsorry! ®

2.31 granting forgiveness
'That's ·all ˌright.
It's 'all ·right ˌnow. ®
It 'doesn't ˌmatter (aˌt all). ®

2.32 expressing approval
ˋGood!
·That's 'fine! ®

2.33 expressing appreciation
(It's) 'very ˌgood/ˌnice.

2.34 expressing regret
'What a ˌpity!
It's a ('great) ˌpity! ®
I'm (so/very) sorry if … ®

2.35 expressing indifference
It ·doesn't ˌmatter.
I don't mind (+ if clause). ®

3 Getting things done (suasion)

3.1 suggesting a course of action (including the speaker)
Let's …
Shall we …? ®

We could ... ®
What about ... (e.g. leaving
now)? ®

**3.2 requesting others to do
something**
Please, ... (e.g. come over here)
..., please.
Will/would/could you ...? ®
Would you mind ...? ®

**3.3 inviting others to do
something**
Would you like to ...?
What about ...? ®

**3.4 accepting an offer or
invitation**
'Thank you.
'Yes, please.
That'll be 'very nice. ®
'All right.

**3.5 declining an offer or
invitation**
'No, thank you.
I'm afraid I cannot ...®

**3.6 enquiring whether an offer or
invitation is accepted or
declined**
Will you ... (do it, come, etc.)?

**3.7 advising others to do
something**
You should ... ®
Why don't you ...? ®

**3.8 warning others to take care
or to refrain from doing
something**
Be ˅careful!
'Look ˅out!
Don't ...
Mind ... (e.g. your head)! ®

3.9 offering assistance
Can I ... (e.g. help you)?

3.10 requesting assistance
Can you ... (e.g. help me),
please?

4   Socialising
(See also Chapter 8 on
sociocultural competence.)

4.1 attracting attention
Ex'cuse ˌme!
Hal˅lo!

4.2 greeting people
'Halˌlo!
'Good ˌmorning/afterˌnoon/
ˌevening.

4.3 when meeting people
'Halˌlo!
'How ˌare you?
(I'm 'fine, ˌthank you,) 'how are
ˌyou?
'How do you ˌdo?
'How do you ˌdo?

4.4 addressing somebody
first name
Mr/Mrs/Miss + family name

4.5 introducing somebody
This is ...

4.6 reacting to being introduced
'Halˌlo.
'How do you ˌdo?

4.7 congratulating
Con'gratuˌlations!

4.8 proposing a toast
'Cheers!
Here's to ... ®

4.9 taking leave
'Goodˌbye.
'Good ˌnight.
I'll ˌsee you (toˌmorrow, ·next
ˌweek, etc.). ®

5   Structuring discourse
(See also Chapter 9.)

5.1 opening
See the exponents of
language functions 4.1, 4.2,
4.4.

5.2 **hesitating, looking for words**
·Er …
'Just a ˌmoment.
'What's the ˌword for it?

5.3 **correcting oneself**
ˌNo, …
ˇSorry, …

5.4 **enumerating**
… and … and …
First …, then …, then …

5.5 **summing up**
So …

5.6 **closing**
·Well, 'good ˌbye/'good ˌnight.
ˋWell, it's been 'nice ˌtalking
with you. ⓑ
I'll 'see you (ˌlater/ˌsoon/
toˌmorrow, etc.) ⓑ

Telephone

5.7 **opening (on lifting the handset)**
telephone number
Oxford 785423
'Halˌlo (this is …)

5.8 **asking for extension**
I'd like to talk to …

5.9 **giving notice of a new call**
I'll 'call aˋgain (ˌlater/this
afterˌnoon, etc.)

Letter

5.10 **opening**
Dear …

5.11 **closing**
Yours sincerely,
Best wishes,
Love from …

6 **Communication repair**
(See also Chapter 10.)

6.1 **signalling non-understanding**
ˇSorry, I 'don't/'didn't
underˌstand (that).
(I ·beg your) 'pardon? ⓑ

6.2 **asking for overall repetition**
(ˇSorry,) 'can you ·say that
aˌgain, ·please?
(I ·beg your) 'pardon? ⓑ

6.3 **asking for partial repetition**
(ˇSorry,) when/where/why/
how/who …?

6.4 **asking for clarification**
(ˇSorry,) 'what is ˌX?

6.5 **asking for confirmation of understanding**
'Did you say ˌX?

6.6 **asking to spell something**
'Can you ˌspell that, ·please?

6.7 **asking to write something down**
'Can you ·write that ˌdown for
me, ·please?

6.8 **expressing ignorance**
I 'don't know ·how to ˌsay it.

6.9 **appealing for assistance**
I ·don't ˋknow the ·English
ˌword.
In [native language] we say …

6.10 **asking to slow down**
'Can you ·speak ˌslowly,
·please?

4 General notions

Introduction

The list of general notions is derived from a consideration of what, in general, people deal with by means of language, of what concepts they may be likely to refer to whatever the specific features of a particular communication situation may be. We present the general notions under eight headings:

1 existential

2 spatial

3 temporal

4 quantitative

5 qualitative

6 mental

7 relational

8 deixis

In the following list we present both the sub-classes of the notions selected and the various notions in the form of their exponents. Strictly speaking, we should have presented each notion and its exponent(s) separately, but since the large majority of the notions would then have to be referred to by means of the corresponding exponent – the lexical item *among* is the exponent of the notion *among* – this would have led to almost constant duplication without any practical gain.

General notions for Waystage including recommended exponents

1 Existential

1.1 *existence, non-existence*
There is …
Is there …?
There's no …
There isn't any …
to make (as in: She 'made a
·new ˌdress.); to become

1.2 *presence, absence*
(not) here, away, (not) there

1.3 *availability, non-availability*
to have (got)
There is …
Is there …?
There's no …
There isn't any …

ready (as in: 'When will it be ˌready?)

1.4 *occurrence, non-occurrence*
to happen

2 Spatial

2.1 *location*
the following adverbs: here, there, nowhere ®, everywhere, somewhere, (not) anywhere, where?; inside, outside
(in) the east/north/south/west
to have been to (as in: He has ·been to ˈParis.)
this, that, these, those

2.2 *relative position*
the following prepositions of position: against ®, among ®, at, at the end of, behind, between, in, in front of, in the centre of, next to, on, opposite ®, under, with.

2.3 *distance*
near
far (away) (from)
… away (as in: It's 'two ˌmiles a·way.)

2.4 *motion*
the following verbs of motion: to come, to come along ®, to come to (as in: He 'came to the ˌhouse.), to fall, to get up, to go, to hurry ®, to leave, to lie down, to pass (as in: You 'pass the ˌrailway ·station.), to sit (down), to stand, to stop (as in: The 'train ˌstopped.)

2.5 *direction*
the following adverbs: away, back, down, in, out, (to the) left, (to the) right, straight on, up,

east (as in: He 'went ˌeast.), north, south, west
the following prepositions: across ®, down ®, from, into, past, through, to, up ®
the following verbs: to bring, to carry ®, to follow, to pull ®, to push ®, to put, to send, to take (as in: I'll 'take it to your ˌroom.), to turn (as in: 'Turn ·left at the ˌriver.)

2.6 *origin*
from (as in: We ·came from ˌLondon.)

2.7 *arrangement*
after (as in: 'B comes ·after ˌA.), before (as in: 'A ·comes before ˌB.), between, first (as in: 'John ·came ˌfirst.), last (as in: 'John ·came ˌlast.)

2.8 *dimension*

2.8.1 size
size (as in: 'What ·size ˌshoes do you ·take?) ®
the following adjectives: big, high, large ®, long, low, short, small, tall ®

2.8.2 length
centimetre, foot, inch, kilometre, metre, mile, yard
long, short

2.8.3 pressure
heavy, light (as in: a light blanket)

2.8.4 weight
gram(me)s, kilos, lbs., oz.
heavy, light

2.8.5 volume
gallon, litre, pint

2.8.6 space
big, small

2.8.7 temperature
temperature ®, degree ®,
zero ®
the adjectives: cold, hot,
warm

3   Temporal

3.1 *points of time*
(three) o'clock, (five) to/past
(three), a quarter to/past (three),
(sixteen) minutes to/past (three),
half past (three)
3 a.m./p.m. ®
noon ®, midnight ®

3.2 *divisions of time*
moment, second ®, minute,
quarter (of an hour), half
(an) hour, hour, day, week,
month, year, century ®;
autumn, spring, summer,
winter; afternoon, evening,
morning, night; weekend,
holiday(s)
names of days of the week,
names of months

3.3 *indications of time*
time (as in: 'What ˌtime is it?)
now, then, when?, soon, ago
(as in: 'two ˌdays ago)
today, tomorrow, yesterday,
the day before yesterday,
the day after tomorrow
this morning/afternoon/
evening/week/month/year;
tonight
last/next + week/month/year
names of days of the week
prepositions: at (as in: at 'three
o'ˌclock), in (as in: in a week; in
1989), on (as in: on Sunday)
dates: (spoken) the first of
June, (written) 1 June 1989
Christmas, Easter

3.4 *duration*
prepositions: **during** ®,
for (as in: for 'three
ˌhours), **since** (as in: since
1945), **till, until** ®
to take (as in: It ·takes
'three ˌhours.) ®
long (as in: a 'long ˌtime),
short

3.5 *earliness*
early (as in: You are ˈearly; an
'early ˌtrain)

3.6 *lateness*
late (as in: We are ˈlate; We
are 'too ˌlate for the ·show;
the ˌlate ·show)

3.7 *anteriority*
present perfect (as in: I
'haven't ·seen ˌJohn ·yet; I've
·been to ˌParis.)
before + NP
before (as in: 'Have you ·been
here beˌfore?) ®
already (as in: I have
al'ready ˌdone it.)
yet (as in: 'Has he ˌcome
·yet?; He 'hasn't ˌcome ·yet.)

3.8 *posteriority*
after + NP
afterwards ®, **later (on)**

3.9 *sequence*
first … then

3.10 *simultaneousness*
at the same time

3.11 *future reference*
NP + *be* going to …
NP + will … ®
soon
in (as in: in 'four ˌweeks)
**next week / month/ year/
Saturday, etc.**
**tonight, tomorrow, the day
after tomorrow, this
afternoon**

3.12 *present reference*
present continuous
simple present
present perfect
now, today, still (as in: He
is 'still ˌworking.)
this morning/afternoon/year
etc.

3.13 *past reference*
past continuous ®
simple past
yesterday, the day before
yesterday, just
last week/month, etc.

3.14 *reference without time focus*
simple present (as in:
'Edinburgh is in ˌScotland.)

3.15 *delay*
late (as in: The ·train is
·going to be 'late.)
delay (as in: There will ·be a
de·lay of 'two ˌhours.) ®
delayed (as in: The 'flight has
been deˌlayed.) ®

3.16 *speed*
fast, slow
… miles/kilometres per hour

3.17 *frequency*
always, never, (not) often,
once ®, sometimes, twice ®,
usually
daily ®, weekly ®, monthly ®
… times a/per week/month,
etc.
on weekdays/Sundays, etc.
every week/Sunday, etc.

3.18 *continuity*
present continuous
past continuous ®
present perfect (as in: I've
·lived ·here for 'two ˌyears.)

3.19 *intermittence*
not always

3.20 *permanence*
always

3.21 *temporariness*
for + NP (as in: for a ˌweek)
not always

3.22 *repetitiousness*
again, many times, twice ®,
several times ®

3.23 *uniqueness*
(only) once ®
(only) one time

3.24 *commencement*
to begin ®, to start
since + NP, from (as in: I ·work
from '9 to ˌ12.)

3.25 *cessation*
to end ®, to stop
till, to (as in: from '9 to ˌ12)

3.26 *stability*
to stay (as in: I am 'going
to ·stay ·here for a ˌweek;
'Will it ·stay ˌdry to·day?)
to wait (as in: We 'had to ·wait
for an ˌhour.)

3.27 *change, transition*
to become (as in: 'Sugar has
be·come exˌpensive.)
suddenly …

4 Quantitative

4.1 *number*
singular/plural
cardinal numerals up to four
digits, ordinal numerals up
to two digits
another (as in: 'May I have
a·nother cup of ˌtea, ·please?)
about (as in: I ·have about ˌ£25.)

4.2   *quantity*
the following determiners: all,
a lot of, (not) any, enough, (a)
few, (a) little, many, more,
most, much, no, some
half (as in: 'Give me ˌhalf of it;
the ˌother ·half; 'half a ˌbottle)
a bottle/cup/glass/piece of …
See further: General Notions
2.8.

4.3   *degree*
comparative and superlative
degrees of adjectives and
adverbs
enough (as in: good enough),
too …, very …
a little (as in: a 'little ˌbetter),
much (as in: 'much ˌbetter)
almost, quite (as in: 'quite
ˌold) ®
rather (as in: 'rather ˌold) ®

5   Qualitative

5.1   *physical*

5.1.1   shape
adjectives: round, square

5.1.2   dimension
See General Notions 2.8.

5.1.3   moisture, humidity
dry, wet
to dry, to make wet

5.1.4   visibility, sight
NP + can(not) see + NP
to look (as in: 'Don't ·look
ᵛnow!), to look at
adjectives: dark, light

5.1.5   audibility, hearing
NP + can(not) hear + NP
to listen, to listen to
noise
loud

5.1.6   taste
nice (as in: This ·meat is 'not
·very ˌnice.)

5.1.7   texture
hard, soft, strong

5.1.8   colour
colour
adjectives: blue, black, brown,
green, grey, orange, red, white,
yellow
light, dark (as in: a light/dark
colour; light/dark blue)

5.1.9   age
age ®
I am … (years old)
How old + *be* + NP?
new, old, young
adult, child; month, year

5.1.10   physical condition
all right, dead, ill, well
to break, to cut, to hurt, to die
to repair

5.1.11   accessibility
to close ®, to open ®
(as in: The ·shop 'opens/'closes
at ˌsix.)
closed/open

5.1.12   cleanness
to clean, to wash
clean

5.1.13   material
nouns and adjectives: gold,
leather, nylon, paper, plastic,
silver
nouns: wood, wool
made of wood, made of wool

5.1.14   fullness
empty, full (of)
to fill

5.2   *evaluative*

5.2.1   value, price
How much + *be* …? (as in:
'How ·much are ·these ˌshoes?)
to be (as in: 'How ·much is
ˌthis?)
price ®
cheap, expensive

5.2.2 quality
adjectives: bad, worse, worst; good, better, best; fine
adverb: well (as in: He 'cannot ˏwrite ·English ·very ·well.)

5.2.3 acceptability
'That's ·all ˏright/ˏfine.

5.2.4 adequacy, inadequacy
NP + *be* all right
NP + *be* (not) enough

5.2.5 desirability, undesirability
to like

5.2.6 correctness, incorrectness
adjectives: better, right, wrong
to be right, to be wrong

5.2.7 capacity, incapacity
NP + can(not) …

5.2.8 importance, unimportance
(not) important

5.2.9 abnormality
strange

5.2.10 facility, difficulty
easy, difficult

6 Mental

6.1 *reflection*
to believe ®, to be sure ®, to be certain ®, to hope, to know, to think, to wonder ®

6.2 *expression*
to ask, to forbid ®, to say, to speak, to talk, to tell, to thank, to write
noun: question

7 Relational

7.1 *spatial relations*
See General Notions 2.2–3, 2.5–7.

7.2 *temporal relations*
See General Notions 3.4–14.

7.3 *action/event relations*

7.3.1 agency
agent as subject
agent in by-adjunct (passive) ®

7.3.2 objective/factitive
objective as object (as in: 'John ·opened the ˏdoor.)
objective as subject of passive (as in: The 'door was ·opened by ˏJohn.) ®
factitive as object (as in: She 'made a ·new ˏdress.)
factitive as subject of passive (as in: 'This caˏthedral | was ·built in the 'thirteenth ˏcentury.) ®

7.3.3 dative
dative as indirect object (as in: He 'gave me a ˏbook.)
dative in to-adjunct (as in: He 'gave the ·ticket to ˏme.)

7.3.4 instrumental
instrumental in with-adjunct (as in: You can 'open the ˏdoor | with 'this ˏkey.)

7.3.5 benefactive
benefactive in for-adjunct (as in: I've 'bought this for my ˏwife.)

7.3.6 place
See General Notions, section 2.

7.3.7 time
See General Notions, section 3.

7.3.8   manner, means
in this way, like this ®
adverbs: **badly, fast, hard**
(as in: to work hard), **how?,**
quickly, slowly, well

7.4   *contrastive relations*

7.4.1   equality, inequality
(not) the same (thing)
different (from), else (as in:
'Anything 'else?) ®, **other,**
another (as in: I want a'nother
ˏroom.)

7.4.2   correspondence, contrast
in addition to the exponents
of 7.4.1:
like (as in: It's ·like an ˏorange.)
comparative degree + than …

7.5   *possessive relations*

7.5.1   ownership, possession
possessive adjectives (**my,**
your, etc.)
possessive pronouns (**mine,**
yours, etc.) (as in: ·This is ˏmine.)
genitive singular of
personal nouns
of-adjuncts, **with-**adjuncts,
without-adjuncts (as in: You
'cannot ·travel here with·out a
ˏpassport.)
to have (got), to get (as in: I ·got
a 'nice ˏpresent from him.**), to**
give, to keep (as in: 'May I ˏkeep
this?)

7.6   *logical relations*

7.6.1   conjunction
and, but
also ®, **too** (as in: ˏJohn is
·leaving | ˏtoo.)

together
pair (as in: a 'pair of ˏshoes),
group (as in: a 'group of
ˏpeople)

7.6.2   disjunction
or

7.6.3   inclusion/exclusion
with (as in: We are 'going
to ·take him ˏwith us.),
without
also ®, **too** (as in: ˏHe is
·leaving | ˏtoo.)

7.6.4   cause
Why …?
because + sub-clause

7.6.5   effect
then …, so … (as in: He ˏate too
·much, | so he 'did not ·feel
ˏwell.)

7.6.6   reason
Why …?
because + sub-clause

7.6.7   purpose
to … (as in: He ·did it to ˏhelp
me.)
in order to … ®

7.6.8   condition
if + sub-clause ®

7.6.9   focusing
about (as in: I 'don't ·want to
ˏtalk a·bout it.)
only (as in: I 'only ·wanted to
ˇhelp.)

8   Deixis

Deixis is the grammatical system for referring or identifying by means of linguistic items belonging to closed sets the reference of which is dependent upon the context of the utterance (e.g. time, place, persons involved). Deixis may be definite or indefinite (*he* vs. *someone*), non-anaphoric or anaphoric (i.e. referring to something mentioned before) (*Why don't you come?* vs. *I'll buy those books because I need them.*).

8.1   *definite*

8.1.1   non-anaphoric
personal pronouns (subject forms and object forms)
possessive adjectives: **my, your**, etc.
possessive pronouns as complement (as in: 'This is ˋmine.)
demonstrative adjectives: **this, that, these, those, such ®**
definite article: **the**
interrogative pronouns: **who, what, which**
interrogative adjectives: **whose ®, what, which**

8.1.2   anaphoric
personal pronouns (subject forms and object forms)
possessive adjectives
possessive pronouns as complement (as in: ˋYou ·take it, | it's ˋyours.)
demonstrative adjectives and pronouns
relative pronouns **®**

definite article: **the**
adverbs: **here, there, now, then, so** (as in: He ˅wanted to ·go, | but he 'didn't ˌsay so.)
propword: **one** (as in: I 'like the ˌred one.)

8.2   *indefinite*
indefinite article: **a, an**
indefinite pronouns: **someone ®, (not) … anyone, nobody ®, something, (not) … anything, nothing, everything, all** (as in: They 'all ·went ˌhome; I ·want ˋall of it.), **some** (as in: 'Some of them ·went ˌhome.), **it** (as in: It's ˌraining.)
adverbs: **everywhere, (not) … anywhere, somewhere, nowhere ®; sometimes, never, always**
semi-deictics: **person** (as in: There were 'five ·persons ˌpresent.), **people** (as in: There were 'many ˌpeople ·present.), **thing** (as in: 'What do you ˌcall that ·thing?), **to do** (as in: 'What are you ·going to ·do toˌnight?)

5 Themes and specific notions

Introduction

Learners who can fulfil the language functions and deal with the general notions listed in Chapters 3 and 4 have a basic potential for using the foreign language for a variety of purposes in a variety of situations. In which situations and for which purposes they can actually do this depends to a large extent on their ability to handle the more specific vocabulary related to particular topics. In the corresponding chapter in *Threshold 1990* (Chapter 7) we listed those themes and specific notions that the learners would be most likely to need to be able to cope with. Since the target group for *Waystage* is substantially the same as that for *Threshold* there is no reason to assume that their needs would be different in this respect. The only difference, in principle, is that at *Waystage* learners will have invested considerably less learning time than at *Threshold*. This will inevitably mean that their sphere of action in the foreign language is more restricted than at *Threshold*. Whereas at *Threshold* learners may be expected to be able to deal with a variety of matters not only in relation to their own individual situation but also in a more generalised, impersonal and occasionally even abstract way, *Waystage* will be largely confined to the personal and the concrete. However, this difference will hardly enable us to effect a considerable reduction in the number of themes and sub-themes selected for *Threshold*. In fact, only a few sub-themes can be eliminated on this basis, notably the ones on 'government and politics' and 'crime and justice'. The reduction which is actually required can only be found in the omission of a large number of specific notions under each of the remaining sub-themes. Doing this will inevitably increase the degree of arbitrariness in the selection, but at least we can attempt to identify, for each sub-theme, a number of notions – and exponents – that may be considered indispensable for coping with it at all. The result of this selection is presented below in the form of lists of those specific notions/exponents that the learners will have to be able to use themselves, productively, if they are to have a minimal coping ability. It goes without saying that, in almost any communication situation, they are likely to be confronted with many more language forms than the ones listed. This means that, as part of their preparation for *Waystage*, the learners will have to be provided with ample opportunity to familiarise themselves with such confrontations and to develop strategies for coping with them. Also, they should be given opportunities for learning to understand many more language forms than they can produce themselves.

The corresponding lists in *Threshold 1990* may be used as sources for those further items that may be usefully included to enhance the learners' receptive ability.

It would be unsatisfactory – and it is unnecessary – to restrict the learners' communicative ability to what we referred to above as 'minimal coping ability' across the whole range of themes and sub-themes. It is therefore recommended that *Waystage* should provide for a higher level of ability with regard to at least a few selected themes or sub-themes. Since this would be largely a matter of a somewhat more comprehensive concrete vocabulary, it ought to be feasible even in courses of comparatively short duration. In principle, the selection of these themes should be left to the learners themselves, but one might suggest that at least one of them should be selected from each of the following areas:

- personal life and circumstances
- living conditions and environment
- occupational activities and interests
- leisure activities and social life.

For a possible content specification of these higher-level themes or sub-themes, the reader is referred to the relevant sets in *Threshold 1990*.

In the following list, the 'specific notions' for *Waystage* are arranged under 13 themes:

1 personal identification

2 house and home, environment

3 daily life

4 free time, entertainment

5 travel

6 relations with other people

7 health and body care

8 shopping

9 food and drink

10 services

11 places

12 language

13 weather

The themes may represent the situational context in which particular transactions take place (e.g. buying something in a shop) as well as topics for communicative interactions (e.g. talking about shopping facilities). Under the title of each theme an indication is given as to what learners at *Waystage* may be expected to be able to do with regard to it. These indications are necessarily incomplete and are to be supplemented from other components of our specification.

The specification contains various open-ended items indicated by italics (e.g. *names of occupations*). In these cases we leave it to materials designers, teachers and learners to identify those specific notions, if any, which suit their own purposes. In order to provide some guidance we add, in a number of cases, some items that might be primarily considered, preceded by 'e.g.'. It should be understood that such examples are merely suggestions and in no way recommended for inclusion in any kind of prescribed syllabus.

A number of items are accompanied by illustrative sentences which are meant to clarify the meaning of the item involved. In cases where there is no such example the item is either unambiguous or the intended meaning follows from the (sub-)theme under which it is included.

List of themes and specific notions for *Waystage* including recommended exponents

1   Personal identification

The learners can say who they are, spell their name, state their address, give their telephone number, say when and where they were born, state their age, sex, say whether they are married or not, state their nationality, say where they are from, what they do for a living, describe their family, state their religion, if any, state their likes and dislikes; elicit/understand similar information from others.

1.1   **name**
name
first name
surname
Mr ...
Mrs ...
Miss ...
Ms ... (writing)
to write
'How do you ˌwrite your ·name?

names of letters of the alphabet
to be
He is 'Bill ˌRobinson.

1.2   **address**
to live
'Where do you ˌlive?
street
road
park

square
number
I ·live at 'number ·fif‚teen.
country
I 'live in the ‚country.
town
village
names of countries

1.3 telephone number
telephone
'Have you got a ‚telephone?
to phone
telephone number
O (as pronounced in
telephone numbers)

1.4 date and place of birth
to be born
I was 'born in ‚London on …
names of the months
the required numerals

1.5 age
See General Notions 5.1.9.

1.6 sex
man
woman
boy
girl

1.7 marital status
(not) married

1.8 nationality
names of nationalities

1.9 origin
to be from …
I am from ‚London.

1.10 occupation
job
names of occupations
names of places of work
e.g. factory, farm, hospital,
office, school, shop

names of occupational
activities
e.g. to buy, to teach, to sell, to
work (as in: I 'work in an
‚office.)
boss
to work
'Where do you ‚work?

1.11 education
school
university
student
to study
to go to (school, university)
names of subjects
e.g. English, history, science,
mathematics

1.12 family
father and mother
husband
wife
child
son
daughter
brother
sister

1.13 religion
church
name of one's own religion,
if any

1.14 likes and dislikes
See Language Functions
2.21–23; objects of likes
and dislikes to be derived
from other themes.

1.15 personal appearance
tall
short
slim
dark
fair
good-looking

2   House and home, environment

The learners can describe a house or flat and the rooms in it, refer to furniture and bedclothes, services and amenities, describe regions (particularly the one where they themselves live); obtain/understand similar descriptions and references from others; exchange views on these matters.

2.1   accommodation, rooms
house
flat
room
names of rooms
e.g. bathroom, bedroom, kitchen, toilet, living-room
floor
The 'bedrooms are on the ·first ˌfloor.
stairs
downstairs
The 'kitchen is ·downˌstairs.
'Let's go ·downˌstairs.
upstairs
The 'bathroom is ·upˌstairs.
'Let's go ·upˌstairs.
lift
window
door
garden

2.2   furniture, bedclothes
furniture
names of pieces of furniture
e.g. bed, chair, table
blanket
pillow
sheet

2.3   services
electricity
gas
heating
telephone
water

on/off
The 'heating is ˌon/ˌoff.
to turn on/off
'How do you ·turn on/off the ˌheating?

2.4   amenities
bath
shower
radio
television
garage

2.5   region
farm
factory
fields
forest
hill
lake
mountain
canal
river
sea
beach
island

2.6   flora and fauna
animal
names of animals
e.g. bird, cat, dog, fly, horse, insect
plant
tree
flower
grass

3   Daily life

The learners can describe their daily routines, at home and at work;
obtain/ understand similar information from others; exchange views
on these matters.

3.1   **at home**
to get up
to have breakfast, etc.
breakfast
lunch
dinner
supper
coffee
tea
to make
'Shall I make ˌtea?
to wash up
to clean
'Who ·cleans the ˌwindows?

to go shopping
to go to school
to go to work
to come home
to go to bed

3.2   **at work** (See also 1.10.)
to work
working hours
holiday(s)
to be free
We are 'free on ˌSaturdays.
colleague
to earn
tax(es)

4   Free time, entertainment

The learners can say when they are free and what they do in their spare
time, particularly with reference to hobbies and interests, public
entertainment, sports and reading; obtain/understand similar
information from others; exchange views on these matters; make use
of entertainment facilities.

4.1   **leisure**
to be free
I'm 'free ·after ˌsix.
holiday(s)
to go out

4.2   **hobbies and interests**
(See also Language Functions
2.21–23.)
hobby
names of hobbies,
particularly one's own
names of fields of interest
e.g. **computers, films, music,**
sports
to go for …
I 'always ·go for a ˌwalk | on
ˌSundays.

4.3   **entertainment**
radio
to listen to (the radio)
television
to watch (TV)
programme
news
film
music
song

4.4   **cinema, theatre**
cinema
theatre
names of public performances
e.g. **film, opera, play, show**
to dance
to sing

to play
She is ·playing in ‚Cats.
He ·plays the gui‚tar.
ticket
'I'll ·get the ‚tickets.

4.5   **intellectual pursuits**
to read
to study
to learn
book

4.6   **sports**
sport(s)
names of sports
e.g. baseball, football, tennis,
swimming

to play
I've 'never ‚played | ‚hockey.
to watch
to win
to lose
against
We 'saw ·England against
‚France | in '6 ‚8.

4.7   **press**
newspaper
magazine
'Let's ·buy some ·maga‚zines.
picture
advertisement

· ·

5   Travel

The learners can use means of public transport, obtain tickets, refer to
means of private transport, make use of the road traffic system, refer to
holiday trips, make use of accommodation facilities for travellers, refer
to travel documents; talk about these matters and activities with
others.

5.1   **public transport**
to go
'How can I ·go to ‚Liverpool?
to travel by air, train, bus, etc.
journey
plane
airport
bus
coach
bus stop
train
underground
'Let's ·take the ‚under·ground.
(railway) station
platform
to change
For 'Leeds you have to ·change
at ‚Sheffield.
tram
tram stop
boat
taxi
ticket

single
'Two ·singles to ‚Brighton,
·please.
return
A re'turn ·ticket is `cheaper |
than 'two ‚singles.
class
I 'always ·travel ‚second ·class.
to smoke
luggage

5.2   **private transport**
(See also 5.3 and 10.7–8.)
bicycle
car
to drive
driver

5.3   **traffic**
street
road
motorway
bridge
crossing

to cross
'Don't ·cross ⱽhere!
corner
traffic lights
common road-sign texts
(reading only)
e.g. cross now, exit, give way,
keep left, keep right, no
parking, no waiting, one way,
stop, turn left, turn right

5.4   holidays
journey
tourist
to visit
names of sights and buildings
of interest
e.g. castle, cathedral, ruins,
zoo
foreign
'Are you ·going to a ·foreign
ˌcountry?

names of countries
names of continents

5.5   accommodation
names of types of
accommodation for travellers
e.g. camping-site, guest house,
hotel, tent
single room
double room
to book
key
bill
'Can I have my ˌbill, ·please?

5.6   luggage
luggage
bag
suitcase

5.7   documents
passport
insurance
driving licence

6   Relations with other people

The learners can refer to personal relations, participate in social life,
deal with matters of correspondence.

6.1   social life
(See also Language Functions
4.1–9.)
friend
colleague
acquaintance
to know (a person)
to make an appointment
to visit
party
We're ·having a 'party | toˌnight.
to talk
to dance
present
He ·brought a ˌpresent ·for me.

6.2   correspondence
(See also Language Functions
5.10–11.)

to write (to)
letter
envelope
postcard
paper
'Have you ·got some ˌpaper ·for
me?
stamp
pen
pencil
ball point
to send
I'll 'send you a ˌpost·card.
to get
I ·got a 'letter from her.
answer
to answer

7   Health and body care

The learners can refer to matters of personal comfort, stating whether
they feel well, are hungry, tired, etc., refer to matters of personal
hygiene and obtain articles required, refer to matters of health and
illness and describe what is wrong to a doctor or dentist, report
accidents, refer to medical services and insurance; obtain/understand
similar information and references from others.

7.1   **parts of the body**
names of parts of the body
e.g. arm, back, foot, hair, hand,
head, heart, leg, neck, stomach,
tooth

7.2   **personal comfort**
to feel well
to look well
hungry
thirsty
tired
to sleep
to wake up

7.3   **hygiene**
comb
razor
soap
toothbrush
towel
to wash
I'd 'like to ˌwash before ·dinner.
'Can you ·wash these ˌclothes
·for me?

7.4   **ailments, accidents**
ill
to feel ill

pain
to have a cold
to hurt
accident
to fall
to break
He has 'broken his ˌleg.
to burn
He has 'burnt his ˌhand.
to cut
She has 'cut her ˌfinger.

7.5   **medical services**
hospital
dentist
doctor
chemist
medicine
'Do you ·take any ˌmedicine?
appointment
'What ·time is your
apˌpointment?
to see a doctor/dentist
glasses

7.6   **insurance**
insurance

··

8   Shopping

The learners can use shopping facilities, particularly obtaining
foodstuffs, clothes and household articles, pay for things bought;
exchange information and views on these matters.

8.1   **shopping facilities**
shop
to go shopping
supermarket
market

to pay (for …)
to buy
to sell
to show

8.2 foodstuffs
See 9.1.

8.3 clothes, fashion
(See also General Notions
2.8.1, 5.1.7–8.)
clothes
names of clothes
e.g. blouse, coat, dress, hat,
raincoat, shirt, shoes, skirt,
socks, tights, trousers,
underwear
to try on
to put on (clothes)
to take off (clothes)
watch
I 'need a ·new ˌwatch.

8.4 household articles
fork
knife
spoon
plate
Be ˇcareful, | the ·plate is ˇhot.
cup
bottle
glass

8.5 prices (See also General
Notions 5.2.1.)
to pay
money
£ (pound)
p (penny, pennies, pence)
names of national currencies

....

9 Food and drink

The learners can refer to and order various kinds of food and beverages,
also in a restaurant, café, etc.; exchange information and views on food,
drink and places for eating and drinking.

9.1 types of food and drink
(See also General Notions
5.1.6.)
food
to eat
meal
snack
to have breakfast/coffee/
lunch/tea/dinner/supper
vegetable(s)
names of vegetables
(to) boil(ed)
(to) fry(ied)
(to) grill(ed)
(to) roast
I'd ·like some 'roast ˌchicken.
salad
meat
names of kinds of meat
fish
chicken
egg
omelette

soup
cheese
mustard
salt
pepper
ice-cream
fruit
names of fruits
bread
butter
piece
'Would you ·like a ·piece of
ˌbread?
slice
sandwich
jam
to drink
coffee
tea
cream
milk
sugar

drink
'Would you ·like a ,drink?
beer
juice
water
wine

9.2   **eating and drinking out**
restaurant
café
pub
menu
bill

10   Services

The learners can refer to, inquire about and make use of postal services, telephone and telegraph, bank, police, medical services, car-maintenance services and petrol stations.

10.1   **post** (See 6.2.)
post office

10.2   **telephone**
See 1.3 and Language
Functions 5.7–9.

10.3   **telegraph**
telegram

10.4   **bank** (See also 8.5.)
bank
to change
I'd ·like to ·change '500 ,francs.
cheque
to cash
I'd 'like to ·cash this ,cheque.

10.5   **police**
police
policeman
police station
to steal
to lose
I've 'lost my ,pass·port.

10.6   **hospital, surgery**
See 7.5.

10.7   **garage**
garage
trouble
engine
lights
brake
to help
to repair
to work
My ,brakes ·don't ·work.

10.8   **petrol station** (See also
General Notions 2.8.5.)
petrol
oil
to check
tyres
full

11   Places

The learners can ask the way and give strangers directions. See General Notions 2.1–5 and Specific Notions 1.2 and 5.3.

12 Language

The learners can refer to foreign language ability and deal with problems of understanding and expression.

12.1
ability, understanding,
expression
See Language Functions
6.1–10 and General Notions
5.2.7 and 5.2.10. In addition:
to read
to speak
to understand
names of languages
e.g. English, French, German,
Spanish
to write

a little
not at all
well
I 'cannot ·write ·English ·very
ˌwell.
dictionary
question
clear
It's 'not ˌclear to me.
to explain
mistake

13 Weather

The learners can obtain relevant information from a weather forecast and exchange information and views on weather conditions.

13.1
weather conditions
weather
sun
rain
to rain
fog
snow
to snow

ice
wind
windy
thunderstorm
fine
It will be ˈfine, | toˌmorrow.

6 Dealing with texts: reading and listening

All the activities listed in the description of the *Waystage* objective (Chapter 1) may be carried out in direct oral contacts. Most of them, however, may also involve a confrontation with written texts or with spoken texts produced through media. In view of the similarity of the communication situations provided for in *Threshold 1990* and in the present objective there is no reason to assume that there will be substantial differences between learners at either level as to the nature of the texts they are likely to need to be able to interpret or as to the kind of understanding that will be required. In both cases the learners will have to be able to 'understand the gist and/or relevant details' of texts relevant to the situations or topics involved in the specification of the objective. This means that, in both cases, they will have to be able to use such interpretation strategies as:

- distinguishing main points and secondary points

- distinguishing fact from comment

- identifying relevant information

- making use of clues such as titles, illustrations, paragraphing, and, in oral texts, structurally relevant pauses, tone of voice, etc.

In both cases, too, the texts to be understood will have to satisfy the following criteria:

- they have a clear structure, both conceptually and formally

- the relevant information contained in them is exclusively or mainly offered explicitly

- their understanding presupposes little or no familiarity with specific features of a foreign culture, other than 'general European culture'

- they are produced in an easily accessible form.

No limitation is put on the kind of information to be understood from a text as defined above. This means that the understanding is not confined to factual information but may equally concern the expression of opinions, attitudes, moods and wishes, provided that particularly the second criterion above is satisfied.

The criteria we have listed are imposed by the limitations of the foreign language ability inherent in early learning objectives. At *Waystage* this ability is more heavily restricted than at *Threshold* and this means that lexically and structurally, as well as conceptually, texts that are understandable at this level are likely to be simpler and easier than those at *Threshold* and that the manner of understanding to be expected will be related to the concrete and personal rather than to the abstract and general.

No indications are given as to the range and nature of the lexical content of texts to be understood. When a learner can use the strategies listed as I.1–5 and II.1–4 in Chapter 10 on 'compensation strategies' there is no point in trying to specify the limits of the vocabulary content that the learners may be supposed to be able to deal with. This is all the more valid for reading if the learners have access to a dictionary and know how to use it.

Although an exhaustive enumeration of text types that, either at *Waystage* or at *Threshold*, the learner will be able to deal with is not possible, we shall list, by way of guidance and exemplification, those text types that at *Waystage* would seem to be particularly relevant in view of the general description of the objective in Chapter 1. By 'relevant' we mean 'relevant to the learner's needs and interests', and the implication of 'at *Waystage*' is that we exclude those text types which would be likely to make a much greater demand on the learners' familiarity with the foreign language than may be expected at this level.

Reading

Text types for reading

Signs (e.g. street signs), directions (e.g. how to make a phone call), notices, instructions (e.g. warnings), posters, advertisements, brochures, leaflets, guides (e.g. hotel guides, city guides), price lists, timetables, bills, tickets, radio/TV/theatre programmes, legends (of maps), telephone directories, forms (e.g. landing forms, hotel registration forms), shop signs, product packaging (e.g. in supermarkets), instructions on automatic vending machines; personal correspondence (letters, postcards, telegrams); informative articles, features, weather forecasts, *from* newspapers and magazines.

Listening

The range of text types proposed for listening is considerably narrower than that for reading. Generally, the understanding of orally produced texts is subject to time constraints: they are produced only once in a linear form which does not allow the listener to go back to earlier parts or to reflect on the text as a whole as easily as may be done with written texts.

In the case of orally produced texts the application of the criterion that they 'are produced in an easily accessible form' is particularly essential. This means that all the texts which the learners are required to be able to understand at *Waystage* should be presented to them with minimal acoustic distortion, in the standard pronunciation or a close approximation of this, and at a speech rate which is in the lower range of what is normal.

Text types for listening

Announcements/information through public address systems at bus stations, railway stations, airports, in flight, in discos, stadiums, at pop concerts, etc.; telephone information (e.g. automatic answering devices: weather, traffic conditions, medical services, timetables, etc.); weather forecasts (radio and TV); traffic information (radio and TV); tourist information (e.g. through portable museum guides); publicity texts (radio, TV, supermarket, etc.); routine commands (instructions/ directions by police, customs officials, airline personnel, etc.).

7 Writing

The text types learners may be expected to be able to produce at *Waystage* may be specified as follows:

1 required data in forms:

- hotel registration forms

- forms required when entering or leaving a country

2 standard letters:

- booking accommodation

3 personal correspondence:

- simple messages such as greetings and congratulations

- simple private letters concerning matters of common interest to themselves and friends or acquaintances.

8 Sociocultural competence

Sociocultural competence is that aspect of communicative ability which concerns those specific features of a society and its culture which are manifest in the communicative behaviour of the members of this society. The degree of familiarity with them which is required for successful communication depends on the circumstances in which the communication takes place. It will probably be higher in contacts with native speakers of the foreign language (especially when the learner is a temporary resident in the foreign country) than when the foreign language is used as *lingua franca*. *Waystage* is designed to suit all types of contacts. This means, on the one hand, that in attempting to indicate what may be expected of a learner at this level we have to focus on the more predictable type of contact, that with native speakers of the foreign language and particularly with such native speakers in their own country. On the other hand it means that an alertness has to be stimulated in the learners to unexpected social differences between their communication partners and themselves. This applies particularly when English is in use as a medium of international communication between non-native speakers from different cultures. Learners cannot take it for granted that their interlocutor will share either their own values, attitudes, beliefs and social conventions or those of Anglo Saxon peoples. They will need to be alert to signs of cultural differences, to be tolerant of such differences and be prepared to operate whatever strategies may be needed to establish a proper basis for communication by raising cultural differences into consciousness.

The specification of sociocultural competence for *Waystage*, which we present below, is deliberately open-ended and exemplificatory, while several items are formulated at a fairly low level of specificity. In this form, we expect, it may best suit the needs and interests of our highly heterogeneous target population and allow further concretisations to be undertaken for each sub-group individually. As for the other components of the present objective, our selection has been made with the utmost economy, taking into account the overall height of *Waystage 1990*.

Parts of the specification of sociocultural competence correspond to most other components of *Waystage* in that they describe what the learners can *do* in the foreign language. Other parts, however, are formulated in terms of the learners' 'awareness of' certain aspects of the foreign culture. An attempt to formulate these parts as well in terms of the learners' behaviour potential would involve choices of such an arbitrary nature that their validity would be unacceptably low.

What specifications in terms of awareness are meant to ensure is that at *Waystage* the learners will have had certain experiences, that they have been confronted with certain features of the foreign culture or

cultures and that they have been led to pay attention to them and to try
and relate them to their own previous experiences. In other words,
these elements of the *Waystage* objective are concerned with learning
experiences that the learner is supposed to have had. What the learners
do with these experiences and how they affect their own attitudes and
behaviour is deliberately left open. This is done to provide the fullest
possible scope for the accommodation of the large variety of emphases
that will be required for different courses, for different types of
learners, and even for individual learners. It is also in view of the
heterogeneity of our target population that we refrain from specifying
any particular English-speaking community whose culture learners
should be confronted with. English is used as a native language in
many different parts of the world and the ways in which it is used will
reflect the specific features of many different cultures. Which of the
various cultures involved the learners will have to be particularly
confronted with, will depend on the learners' own circumstances.
What is important for all learners is that they should be aware of
possible differences between their own culture and that of others and
that they should have developed the attitudes and acquired the means
for coping with such differences.

Sociocultural competence for English at *Waystage*

I   Social conventions

1   non-linguistic

The learner is aware of the diversity of conventions in different
countries with regard to body language, e.g. hand shaking, touching,
embracing, kissing, gesticulation, close physical proximity and
protracted direct eye contact, and is aware of the embarrassment that
may be caused by non-observance of the conventions followed by the
interlocutor.

2   linguistic

The learner is aware of the conventions governing the performance of
the language functions listed in this document, particularly 4.1–9
(socialising) and those concerning thanking and apologising (2.29–30),
making requests (3.2), accepting and declining (3.4–5), opening and
ending conversations (5.1, 5.6) and is able to act in accordance with
them.

II   Social rituals

....

1   visiting rituals

The learners know – *or can enquire*:

- whether they are expected to be punctual;
- whether they are expected to bring a present, and if so, what sort of present;
- what sort of clothes to wear;
- whether to expect refreshments, or a meal, if asked for a certain time.

....

2   eating and drinking rituals

The learners are aware that rituals may differ from what is customary in their own country, and are ready to observe and, if appropriate, follow others' examples.

....

3   acceptance and refusal rituals

The learners are aware:

- that a first refusal need not be definitive, that, in fact, it may denote a wish to be asked again;
- that, especially in an American context, a suggestion for further contact, or even an invitation, may be just a polite way of ending a contact.

III   Universal experiences

....

1   everyday life

The learners have some familiarity with:

- at what times people have their regular meals and in what ways the composition of meals, including beverages, typically differs from that in their own country;
- major national holidays;
- working hours;
- preferred leisure activities (to the extent that generalisation is possible).

2 living conditions

The learners have some familiarity with:

- living standards, including significant differences between major parts of a country;
- ethnic composition of the population.

3 interpersonal relations

- relations within the family;
- relations between the sexes;
- formality/informality in social contacts, in work situations and in contacts with officials.

4 major values and attitudes

The learners are aware of potential differences from their own culture with regard to the value generally attached to and the prevalent attitude towards e.g.

- social class;
- wealth and security;
- tradition;
- national identity and foreigners;
- interracial relations;
- politics;
- religion.

It should be noted that the list under III.4 is offered by way of exemplification only. It would be unrealistic to assume that all these matters could be dealt with in a *Waystage* course – beyond the stimulation of awareness that different cultures may also differ with regard to 'major values and attitudes'.

In addition to what is specified above, *Waystage* contains a further, implicit, component of sociocultural competence, which is most easily identifiable in the recommended word list. Several items in this list have a meaning which is more or less subtly different from that of their translation equivalents in other languages. For English, *tea* is an obvious example, but also such items as *church*, *soldier*, *town*, *vegetables* may not fully correspond in meaning to comparable words in other languages. At *Waystage* the learner cannot be expected to be aware of all these differences, except to the extent that awareness of them is essential to successful communication within the contexts included in the general description of the objective.

9 Verbal exchange patterns

Exponents of single language functions may occur in isolation. 'Stop!' as an order, and 'Look out!' as a warning, are obvious examples. On the whole, however, function exponents are more likely to occur in sequences. Such sequences will usually exhibit certain regularities in the order of their elements. Thus, an apology will very often be followed by an explanation: 'I'm sorry I'm late, but I had to see my dentist first.' Such more or less regularly occurring combinations may be referred to as *patterns*. Monologues may be thus patterned, if only in that they may start with an utterance calling for attention and end with one signalling termination. With regard to oral communication involving contributions by the learner, the emphasis, at *Waystage*, is not so much on monologues as on verbal exchanges between two, or more than two, speakers. In such exchanges the participants may mesh their contributions in accordance with certain conventions. We then speak of *verbal exchange patterns*. It is a characteristic of these patterns that they are variable, in that a conversation may move in various directions. Especially when they are very short, however, involving only two or three utterances, they may also be standardised. This may be said, for instance, of the typical greeting + response pattern occurring when two people pass each other in the street. The large majority of the verbal exchange patterns, however, that are relevant to *Waystage* learners in the light of the objective are variable. We may illustrate this by reproducing two examples of 'predictable fish-and-chip discourses' provided by A. J. Peck in an article called 'Some ideas on teaching discourse synthesis'. (The function labels are ours.)

1	Sales person	: 'Yes?	asking for wish (opening)
	Customer	: 'Haddock and ˌchips.	expressing wish
	Sales person	: ·That'll be '£1.ˌ20.	asking for payment
	Customer	: (gives money)	(making payment)
	Sales person	: ˌThanks.	thanking (termination)
2	Sales person	: 'Yes?	asking for wish (opening)
	Customer	: 'Fish and ˌchips | – ˌtwice.	expressing wish
	Sales person	: 'Cod, | or ˌplaice?	asking for preference
	Customer	: ˌPlaice.	expressing preference
	Sales person	: 'Large, | or ˌsmall?	asking for preference
	Customer	: ˌLarge.	expressing preference
		And 'salt and ˌvinegar.	expressing further wish

Sales person	: ·That'll be '£2.,30	asking for payment
Customer	: (gives money)	(making payment: non-verbal termination)

Apart from the variability (by no means exhausted here) of the 'fish-and-chip buying dialogue', we note the occurrence of sub-patterns as well as the integration of non-verbal turns. Communicative ability at *Waystage* implies the ability to play a part in verbal exchange patterns such as the ones illustrated above.

A number of dialogue types (which may, in fact, involve more than two participants) are explicitly or implicitly covered by our objective. They involve the occurrence of verbal exchange patterns with a certain measure of predictability. They are particularly associated with the following communicative events:

1 making purchases

   a) in a shop

   b) at a ticket counter, ticket from bus conductor, etc.

2 ordering food and drink
   restaurant, canteen, snack bar, etc.

3 making enquiries

   a) non-personal (where to go, where to eat, about opening hours, about various facilities and services, etc.)

   b) personal (about name, address, place of origin, etc.)

4 meeting people

   a) strangers

   b) friends, acquaintances

5 asking and showing the way

6 asking and telling the time

7 inviting and reacting to invitation

8 arranging accommodation

9 proposing a course of action and reacting to such proposals

10 having a discussion
   agreeing/disagreeing, exchanging views, etc.

However predictable the occurrence of certain verbal exchange patterns in the above dialogue types may be, there is always a strong element of unpredictability as well. When the more or less standardised patterns are broken, or even set aside completely, conversation does not lend itself to a didactically meaningful description of the kind we try to provide in this document. 'All we can be said to understand about such talk,' Peck observes, 'is that certain elements occur frequently. These act as signposts along a road we are travelling.' He adds: 'We can teach pupils to recognise these elements of discourse and to use them themselves.'

Chapter 3 contains a classified list of the language functions, together with their common exponents, which are combined in verbal interaction. We have not thought it necessary, or even desirable, to attempt to specify the verbal interaction patterns to be used by learners (e.g. in the form of praxeograms).

As we have shown, not even the most routine transactions of daily life are fully predictable. Many conditions may have to be fulfilled before a transaction can be successfully completed. A complex transaction may have to pass through numerous stages of negotiation each involving lengthy verbal exchanges. In routine cases many may be passed over in silence and the exchange limited to a few words on either side. Making travel arrangements, say, may take either form. We all know what it is like to queue behind someone who wishes to travel to a remote place involving different means of transport, choices of route, co-ordination of timetable, comparison of prices using different combinations of various categories of tickets, involving different currencies, wishing to use a foreign credit card, etc., when all one wishes to do oneself is to buy a single ticket to the next station, and the train is due to leave in five minutes. One wishes there were simply a ticket vending machine, in which case no oral interaction need – or indeed can – take place, but instead a set of written instructions must be followed. The example could be paralleled in the settings of shopping, eating out, garages, and others where goods and services are required. In each case the services and/or goods must be identified, made available and paid for. Each stage may be carried out through personal interaction involving more or less verbal interaction or by self service with or without mechanisation, normally eliminating verbal interaction in favour of written instructions. What is to be done at each stage may be self-evident, requiring no language, or a perfunctory exchange, or a brief unrelated interactional exchange to establish human contact. On the other hand, there may be choices to be exercised, preferences to be expressed, pros and cons to be discussed, conflicts of interest to be resolved, before the decisions can be made on which the next stage depends. At any time, communication difficulties may arise, needing to be dealt with by repair procedures. As social beings we have the larger schemata in our social competence, though it is only in exceptional circumstances that we need to follow the full process through in detail by means of language. In any case:

- the schemata are largely shared by European societies. Where transactions and interactions are governed by different rules, effective communication and co-operation depend, of course, on mutual understanding between participants from different backgrounds (e.g. whether and how bargaining is conducted over prices, whether tipping is expected for small services, etc.);

- the order in which the steps occur is not altogether fixed;

- whether steps are made explicit or passed over in silence depends on the situation and on cultural conventions;

- the ways in which objects are identified, preferences expressed, dissatisfaction or agreement shown and so on are not specific to particular situations (beyond the topic-specific words and expressions required). They are generalisable as resources which can be called on according to need in a wide range of situations. It is this principle which underlies the notional/functional approach as distinct from some other situational approaches.

For these reasons, we do not specify here in an exhaustive way the patterns of verbal interaction which a learner should be able to carry through in the situations envisaged. To attempt to do so would be at once too restrictive and over elaborate. In some cases (e.g. *having a discussion*) the possibilities of combining speech acts are virtually unlimited. In others (e.g. *asking and telling the time*) a two-term exchange normally suffices, apart from non-specific opening and closing exchanges. A general schema, such as that presented below, may however be set up to cover, with certain adaptations, the various transactions involving the purchase of goods and services.

General Schema for purchase of goods or services

1 Moving to place of transaction

    1.1 finding the way to the shop, store, supermarket, restaurant, station, hotel, etc.

    1.2 finding the way to the counter, department, table, ticket office, reception, etc.

2 Establishing contact

    2.1 exchanging greetings with the shopkeeper/assistant/waiter/ receptionist, etc.

        2.1.1 assistant greets

        2.1.2 customer greets

3 Selecting goods/services

   3.1 identifying category of goods/services required

      3.1.1 seeking information

      3.1.2 giving information

   3.2 identifying options

   3.3 discussing pros and cons of options (e.g. quality, price, colour, size of goods)

      3.3.1 seeking information

      3.3.2 giving information

      3.3.3 seeking advice

      3.3.4 giving advice

      3.3.5 asking for preference

      3.3.6 expressing preference
           etc.

   3.4 identifying particular goods required

   3.5 examining goods

   3.6 agreeing to purchase

4 Exchanging goods for payment

   4.1 agreeing prices of items

   4.2 agreeing addition of total

   4.3 receiving/handing over payment

   4.4 receiving/handing over goods (and receipt)

   4.5 exchanging thanks

      4.5.1 assistant thanks

      4.5.2 customer thanks

5 Leave taking

   5.1 expressing (mutual) satisfaction

      5.1.1 assistant expresses satisfaction

      5.1.2 customer expresses satisfaction

   5.2 exchanging interpersonal comment (e.g. weather, local gossip)

   5.3 exchanging parting greetings

      5.3.1 assistant greets

      5.3.2 customer greets

It will be seen that the sequence is not strictly linear. In hotels and restaurants 4.4 may come between 3.4 and 3.5, payment being made normally at the end of the meal or period of residence. In a village shop elements of 5.2 may be interspersed with any of the other stages. In the case of supermarkets and especially mechanised vending machines 2 and 5 do not apply. 3.1–3.6 and 4.3–4.4 are carried out in silence by the customer in 'dialogue' with written descriptions and instructions – a process often preferred by foreign visitors and even native speakers as avoidance strategies against expected difficulties of interpersonal communication.

It will also be seen that (4) is central. A minimal interaction consists of 4.4 and 4.5, performed by actions without words.

Peck 1: 3.1.1–3.4–4.1–(4.3 and 4)–4.5.1

Peck 2: 3.1.1–3.1.2–3.2–3.4–3.2–3.4–3.4–4.1–(4.3)–(4.4)

Peck's examples are brief and businesslike, in a situation where choice is extremely restricted and prices are fixed. Other situations (e.g. a celebratory meal in an expensive restaurant, buying an expensive dress in a prestigious store) would call on more of the resources implied, as might the selection of hotel accommodation or the kind of complex travel arrangements outlined earlier.

10 Compensation strategies

No matter how hard we try to assess and to predict learners' communication needs, to determine the situations requiring foreign language use which they are most likely to find themselves in, and to identify those language forms which are most likely to enable them to cope with these situations, there will always be a very broad margin of unpredictability. And even if the demands of a particular communication situation do not exceed that which the learners have been thoroughly prepared for, there are likely to be failures of recall, failures to activate, on the spur of the moment, certain items of knowledge or elements of skill that were acquired during the learning process.

This means that even if we confine ourselves to the requirements of everyday situations, predictable to a certain extent, the learner has to be prepared to cope with unpredicted demands as well as with failures of recall.

To some people skill in coping comes naturally. Somehow they manage, whatever their lack of skill or knowledge with regard to the 'proper' forms of communication. Most people, however, will benefit substantially by being given ample opportunity, in the course of their learning process, to develop their skill in this respect. It is not primarily a matter of being 'taught' how to cope, but of being led to develop one's own strategies for doing so. Although certain strategies and techniques may almost certainly be beneficial to everyone, individual differences corresponding to differences in personality are to be given full scope.

What may be expected of learners at *Waystage*, then, is some skill in dealing with the demands of a communication situation that they are not fully prepared for. This means particularly that:

   as a reader or listener the learner is not 'thrown' by the occurrence of unknown linguistic elements in a text;

   as a speaker or writer the learner is prepared to seek solutions to problems caused by insufficient linguistic skill or knowledge;

   as a social agent the learner is not put out by uncertainty as to the accepted code of behaviour.

There is no direct relationship between these attitudinal aspects and specific abilities. Different learners are likely to develop different sets of strategies for coping with the problems involved. Consequently, no standard operationalisation is to be sought. Yet, among the various techniques and strategies that are available a certain number may be identified as particularly likely to suit each individual learner and to contribute substantially to the development of the desired attitudes.

Like other aspects of communicative ability at *Waystage*, this may be described and listed in terms of what the learner can do, and supplemented with recommended exponents where this is appropriate. Because some items will involve the fulfilling of particular language functions and the handling of particular notions, a partial overlap with other lists in the present objective is inevitable. A similar overlap will occur between the present list and that of the chapter on 'dealing with texts' (Chapter 6).

I As a reader, the learner can:

1 deduce the meanings of complex words composed of elements (base(s) and affixes) which are familiar to the learner and which are combined in accordance with productive rules of word formation, insofar as these meanings are directly derivable on the basis of familiarity with the elements involved and with generally applied rules of word formation;

2 deduce the meanings of unfamiliar elements (particularly phrases and words) from a context of familiar elements which allows these meanings to be identified;

3 correctly interpret the meanings of so-called 'international words' that are familiar from the learner's native language and whose formal relation to the native language equivalent is fully transparent; he/she is aware of the existence of 'false friends' and will remain on the alert for differences in the meanings of 'international' words and cognate words from one language to another;

4 find the meanings of unknown words or phrases in a bilingual dictionary or alphabetically arranged word list as well as in a monolingual dictionary, provided that the defining vocabulary contains mostly familiar elements;

5 with or without the aid of the above devices derive specific information from a text containing unknown elements, provided that, in addition to what is specified elsewhere in the present objective, this does not require further abilities than those listed above, the acceptable degree of difficulty of the text depending on the availability or non-availability of a dictionary or word list.

II As a listener, the learner can:

1 carry out the operation described in I.1, provided that the word-formation process involved does not entail further phonological changes in the constituent elements than linking, stress adjustment, and consequent (regular) vowel and consonant changes;

2 carry out the operation described in I.2, provided that the contextual clues are presented in such a way that they are recognisable as such and interpretable in linear sequence without necessitating backtracking and reconsideration of the context;

3 carry out the operation described in I.3, provided that phonological differences between the foreign language form and the native language form are confined to standard correspondences between the two languages;

4 derive specific information from a text containing unknown elements, provided that, in addition to what is specified elsewhere in the present objective, this does not require further abilities than those listed in II.1, II.2 and II.3;

5 in face-to-face contacts appeal to a communication partner's assistance, particularly by using the devices listed in section 6 of Language Functions.

III As a speaker, the learner can:

1 introduce a rephrasing

(ˇSorry,) I'll 'start aˌgain.
(ˇSorry,) I'll 'try to ·say that aˌgain.

2 describe by means of paraphrase, particularly by using a general word (person, thing, etc.) or a superordinate, together with a qualification indicating:

– general physical properties such as colour, size, shape (See General Notions.)

– specific features (a ·thing with 'three ˌlegs)

– use ('something to ˌsit on)

3 describe by referring to qualities and properties:

– general physical properties (See General Notions.)
It is ·made of ˌwood.

– specific features
It has 'three ˌlegs | and 'no ˌback.

– use
You ˌsit on it.

4 identify by indicating

one ·like ˌthat
I'd ·like ˌthis, ·please.

5 appeal for assistance
'What do you ,call ·that (a·gain)?
I 'don't ·know the ·English/·German, **etc.** ,word.
In [native language] we say ...

IV   **As a writer,** the learner can:

1 express ignorance
I 'don't ·know ·how to ,say it.
I 'don't ·know ·what you ,call it.

2 use the devices mentioned under III.2 and III.3;

3 use dictionaries, both bilingual and monolingual of an appropriate
kind.

V   **As a social agent,** the learner can:

1 apologise for uncertainty or ignorance as to the accepted code of
behaviour
I'm ˅sorry | I 'don't/'didn't ,know ...

2 refer to what is customary in his/her own country
In ˅my ·country we ...

3 ask for guidance
'How is this ,done in ·your ·country?
'How should I ,do this?
'What should I ,do?
At 'what ·time should I ,come?
etc.

The above strategies and techniques are those that every learner at
Waystage may be expected to be able to use in association with the use
of the language functions listed in section 6 of Chapter 3. In addition,
each individual learner is likely to have other privileged devices at his
or her disposal. They may, but will not necessarily, include such
techniques as finding information in grammatical surveys, in general
reference works, etc., and such strategies as using a synonym for an
unknown word, allowing oneself to use grammatically imperfect
forms, experimenting with word formation, foreignising a native-
language form, etc. Which of these devices the learners are given
opportunities to adopt cannot be laid down in a general objective but is
to be left to those providing learning facilities.

11 Learning to learn

Waystage is an objective derived from the estimated needs of the learners as communicators. A course – that is the sum total of the learning experiences offered to the learners – designed for *Waystage* will have to enable the learners to satisfy these needs. Yet, it will inevitably do other things as well. Depending on its design and presentation it may give the learners pleasure or hardship, it may promote, maintain, or reduce their motivation for learning, it may bolster or diminish their self-confidence, it may stimulate their interest and sensitivity to the world around them or it may cause them to withdraw into themselves. In short, it may benefit the learners far beyond the basic objectives of the course or it may limit itself to this and, possibly, it may even harm the learners as persons. All these effects – positive or negative – are independent of the learning load that is represented by the content of an objective; they are produced by the impact upon particular learners of the forms and the manners of the presentation and the practice of this content. At the same time they may affect the learners' impression of the learning load in making this load appear to be more demanding or less so.

The experience, then, of learning for *Waystage* will affect the learners in various ways beyond the acquisition of a certain learning content. One of the ways in which it may substantially benefit the learners is in stimulating their awareness of the learning process itself and increasing their learning potential. This 'learning to learn' does not, at first sight, appear to fall within our communicative objective. It may, however, easily be integrated into this objective. And there are at least two good reasons for trying to do so. In the first place, it has now long been accepted by learning psychologists that insightful learning is likely to be more effective – and to produce more lasting effects – than learning without insight. This greater effectiveness is partly due to the motivating power of knowing what one is doing and why one is doing it. Secondly, 'learning to learn' is an invaluable aspect of preparing the learners for whatever further learning may be required by them. Like any general objective, *Waystage* is no more than an assessment of what the average member of a particular target group is most likely to need at a given stage in his or her development. The actual needs of individual members of the target group are certain to differ to a greater or a lesser extent from those of the fictitious 'average member'. This means that in order to be adequately equipped for independent functioning in and with the foreign language, learners should have the insights and know-how required for bridging the gap between their individual needs and those provided for in the specifications of the general objective. And even if the gap is so wide that the learners may have to seek professional guidance, some insight into their own learning potential and how to exploit this most effectively will be of considerable advantage to them.

Finally it should be said that the promotion of learner autonomy is a fundamental objective of the communicative approach adopted by the Council of Europe. That is to say the learners should be encouraged and enabled to take increasing charge of their own learning and to develop the attitudes, knowledge, understanding and skills which will enable them to do so. Insofar as *Waystage* is the statement of a learning objective and not just a description of a certain level of proficiency, the skills involved in learning to learn are not simply a by-product of some courses, but an essential aspect of that objective, which all teaching towards that objective should promote. As such they form an integral part of the objective, not an optional extra.

Thus, in describing what learners should be able to do with and through the use of language for communication, we legitimately take into account their use of the experience of language learning to become more efficient and effective language learners as well as language users. It is part of the *Waystage* objective for learners to be willing and able to engage in the struggle to communicate in the situations confronting them with the resources and strategies they command, taking the risk of error, inviting and welcoming various forms of assistance from more experienced interlocutors and, systematically, to learn from the experience. It is also part of the objective that learners should actively seek opportunities for engaging in such encounters, exploiting not only the presence of native speakers in the environment but also the opportunities offered by radio and television broadcasts as well as printed and recorded material.

'Learning to learn', as we said above, should be incorporated into the *Waystage* objective, not as an additional objective that will affect the pragmatic/linguistic content but as one that is to be achieved through the form and manner of presentation and practice of this content or, indeed, through the individual's experience of the language. We shall formulate the learning-to-learn component in terms of a learning objective, but at a fairly high level of generality, leaving scope for a range of concrete realisations by individual learners with possibly different learning styles.

The 'learning-to-learn' objective

I   Concerning needs and objectives

1 The learners are aware of the nature of their communicative needs.

2 The learners are aware of the nature of the learning objective offered to them.

3 The learners have insight into the degree of relevance to their communicative needs of the learning objective offered to them.

4 In the areas covered by the open categories of Chapter 5 (Specific notions) the learners are able to identify, learn and use the terms specific to their own nationality, employment, leisure interests, etc.

5 The learners can identify those of their communicative needs, if any, which are not catered for in the objective offered to them.

6 The learners can describe, in general terms, additional objectives which will satisfy the needs referred to under 5 above and/or they can recognise the relevance to these needs of further objectives offered to them, for example:

> I'd 'like to ·read ·articles about eco‚nomics.
> I'd 'like to ·write ‚business ·letters.

II Concerning learning processes

1 The learners are familiar with the possibility of dividing an overall learning task into a number of sub-tasks, each with its own objective.

2 The learners are familiar with the distinction between productive ability and receptive ability and with the difference in degree of skill that may be required in order to meet the needs for each type of ability.

3 The learners are aware of the contributions of pragmatic, grammatical, lexical and phonological adequacy to communicative effectiveness.

4 The learners can identify the roles (acquisition of knowledge, of insight, of skill) of various types of learning materials and are aware of the potential relevance of such materials to the achievement of their objective.

5 The learners know how to find information about usage (e.g. in dictionaries, relevant reference works and reference grammars designed for use by non-advanced learners).

6 The learners have experienced various methods of vocabulary acquisition and have identified one or more that they consider particularly useful to themselves.

7 The learners are aware of the potential of learning through exposure to foreign language use and know how various compensation strategies may enable them to cope with texts containing unknown elements.

III Concerning learning from direct experience of the language

1 The learners are able to engage in communicative interaction using the resources and strategies specified at *Waystage* and to learn from experience.

2 The learners are able to observe the language and strategies used by a more experienced interlocutor and thus increase their own repertory of responses, receptive and productive.

3 The learners are, for instance, able as listeners and as readers to perceive, memorise and note down words and expressions not previously encountered, noting also their situational context and functional/notional value.

4 The learners are able to repeat back new words and expressions which occur in conversations in which they participate, to make use of them themselves as soon as appropriate and, by later making notes if necessary, add them to their repertory.

5 The learners are able to experiment with forms of expression (e.g. by re-combining known words and grammatical structures, or rules of word and structure formation), to note their acceptance or non-acceptance by more experienced speakers and, if need be, to modify the rules they operate.

6 The learners are able to employ compensation and repair strategies (cf. section 6 of Chapter 3) noting, learning and using new language supplied by their interlocutor.

IV Concerning evaluation

1 The learners can monitor their progress towards the terminal objective, particularly by relating their communicative ability to successive intermediate objectives.

2 The learners are aware of the role of formative assessment as an aid to the planning of further learning activities.

The above analysis of 'learning to learn' is based on assumptions as to what may reasonably be expected to be feasible for learners at an early stage of foreign language learning without diverting too much of their attention from the actual task of learning to use the language itself.

Some learners may well find further items useful, such as ability to consult a reference grammar designed for use by non-advanced foreign learners. It is for the student, preferably with the advice of the teacher, to decide whether its use would facilitate learning at this level or require an expenditure of time and energy incommensurate with the modest requirements of the *Waystage* objective itself.

Several of the above items are formulated as 'the learners are aware of ...'. This obviously allows for different degrees of awareness, and no attempt is made to operationalise this concept. This simply means that, in our view, courses meant to lead up to *Waystage* should provide learners with the opportunity to develop the awareness concerned without, however, making any specific demands upon the learners in this respect.

12 Degree of skill

So far, in the present study, we have been concerned with what learners might have to be able to do in the foreign language in order to satisfy their needs and interests. What we have not dealt with is *how* they should be able to do all the things specified. We have – it is true – listed many exponents (language forms) and strategies that, together, might enable the learners to function economically and effectively in the situations they are most likely to find themselves in. However, the exponents have been offered merely by way of recommendation and the strategies have mostly been described in an open-ended manner.

All this is tantamount to saying that the level we have described is not uniform and fixed but that it allows of many different concretisations in accordance with the diversity of sub-groups and individual members of the target population. Consequently, it is not in itself either a testing syllabus or a course design. However, its high degree of explicitness allows it to be used as a basis for these. A test syllabus designer will then have to determine the exact nature of the concretisations that correspond to the purposes of the test envisaged and thus establish the criteria the learners will have to satisfy in order to pass the test.

Waystage 1990, then, is simply a learning objective, an aim to be pursued with and by the learners and which is specified in such a way that it can give meaningful direction to the planning of learning activities. It is not to be confused with actual learning effects. These will always differ from what is described in an objective. The extent of the difference that is acceptable is primarily a matter for individual learners to decide in accordance with their own needs and ambitions.

Consequently, in dealing with the question *how* and particularly *how well* the learners should be able to do what is specified in this objective we cannot go beyond very general statements which mainly concern minimal requirements for effective communication.

An attempt at communication is effective if the intention of a communicative act is realised. This is the case if the communicator is successful in conveying his or her intention to others and also in correctly interpreting others' intentions that may be relevant to his or her own situation. This means that the main criterion to be applied is *pragmatic adequacy*. If a learner means to apologise humbly or to express doubt he/she communicates effectively if a communication partner understands that he or she is apologising humbly or expressing doubt. And if a learner wants to find out whether or not to wear a raincoat he/she is an effective communicator if he/she correctly interprets the relevant information in a weather forecast.

However, we should not jump to the conclusion that a learner who communicates successfully on one particular occasion has established his or her credentials as a good communicator and has reached the *Waystage* objective. Under favourable circumstances (a constraining situation and an alert, experienced and sympathetic native listener) communication may be unaffected by even gross phonetic, grammatical and lexical distortion. Speech recognition experiments show the great effect of the listener's expectations on identification. The same utterance may well fail to communicate under less constraining circumstances (if, say, the referent is unobservable and not deducible from context) or if the listener is less motivated or less experienced. In particular, non-native listeners are less able to cope with deviance than native speakers. This point is of particular relevance when English is used as a means of communication between non-native speakers of different mother tongues. A level of mother tongue interference which does not interfere seriously with communication with native speakers or with others who have the same mother tongue background may make conversation impossible, or lead to misunderstandings with serious consequences (e.g. where safety or security are involved) where the listener has to rely on the accurate identification of what has been said.

Thus, verbal communication cannot be reasonably assured without at least an approximation to certain grammatical, lexical and phonological norms. This means that errors in these areas that interfere with communicative effectiveness are not acceptable. This conclusion does not, however, automatically lead to the establishment of lists of acceptable and unacceptable deviations from norms.

By definition, any failure to distinguish phonemic pairs, or grammatical categories (e.g. tense/aspect distinctions), is capable of leading to misunderstanding, but the factors which decide whether or not it does so are so complex as to defy quantification. In a high proportion of cases listeners (especially native listeners) will be aware that the speech is deviant, but will understand what the speaker intends. Whether or not such errors are accepted in an otherwise successful communicative act depends on other considerations than those inherent in the present objective. Largely, this is a matter of the learners' personality and their ambitions. A naturally shy person may be severely handicapped as a communicator by being conscious of frequently producing incorrect forms. And one who needs full acceptance as a communication partner in an environment that is intolerant of any manifestation of reduced competence will also need a higher degree of skill than many other learners. *Waystage*, as specified in this document, does not in any way preclude the development of such a higher degree of skill but it does not require it of all the learners within its target group.

Yet it will be to all learners' advantage to set their sights a little higher than just 'pragmatic adequacy'. They should also aim at the ability to communicate with a certain degree of *efficiency*. Speakers who, when giving information about something, have to pause after every second word in order to find a way to continue, who make numerous grammatical and/or lexical mistakes even in short utterances, whose pronunciation does not conform to any standard their communication partner may be familiar with, etc., cannot be said to communicate efficiently because they put a great strain on those listening to them and run the risk of losing their audience altogether.

There is a similar lack of efficiency when listeners, in order to understand what is said to them, need constant repetition or oblige speakers to speak with unnatural slowness or to rephrase their sentences all the time so as to express themselves within an inadequately narrow range of vocabulary and grammar. It may be expected, then, at *Waystage*, that, within the limits set by *Waystage* content:

– *as speakers* the learners can make themselves easily understood not only by listeners with native or near-native command of the language, but also under normal conditions by other non-native speakers who have reached *Waystage*;

– *as listeners* the learners can understand the essence of what is said to them not only by speakers with native or near-native command of the language, but also under normal conditions by other non-native speakers who have reached *Waystage*, without obliging the speakers to exert themselves unduly.

What was said of the learners as speakers will equally apply to the learners as writers. As writers, however, the learners are likely to wish to satisfy somewhat higher criteria of formal correctness, particularly in letters to strangers. Having access to appropriate reference works will enable them to satisfy such criteria more easily than in the production of spoken language.

In all that is said above with regard to efficiency of communication it is to be understood that a certain tolerance and co-operation is expected of the learners' communication partners. It would be unrealistic to assume that at *Waystage* the learners would be able to function adequately without this. Ability to function in more demanding situations as well does not necessarily require further learning efforts but will develop gradually as learners use the language in practice.

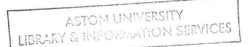

Appendix A   Pronunciation and intonation

Communication depends upon mutual intelligibility. That is to say that it is only possible if the language forms produced by the speaker are identified and understood by the listener. It is therefore the responsibility of speakers to pronounce them as intelligibly as possible, and it is also the responsibility of listeners actively to seek to identify what has been said and to use appropriate repair procedures if they are unable to do so. The ease of communication depends largely on the extent to which speaker and listener share a common practice. Speakers of the same dialect understand each other without difficulty, but widely separated dialects may well be mutually unintelligible. For purposes of national (or international) communication standard languages with standard pronunciations have generally developed, based usually on the speech of educated people in capital cities, or that of some other prestigious social group. The standard language is widely used in the education system, in the serious media and in middle-class life and culture. This is not to say that all users of a standard pronunciation sound alike. The speaker's socio-regional provenance may be clearly marked and easily detectable by an experienced listener. It may well be important to the individual's sense of identity that this should be so (e.g. Scottish English), but conformity to national norms is sufficient to ensure ready mutual intelligibility on a national scale. In Britain, this role is played by Received Pronunciation (RP) as codified by D. Jones, A.C. Gimson and others, and generally adopted by broadcasting authorities, dictionary makers, language course designers, etc. In its pure form, RP is the practice of a small but influential minority, but with increasing mobility and media exposure a high proportion of speakers use, either habitually or as required, a regionally coloured approximation to RP which is universally intelligible. Regional variants differ mainly in vowel colouring. The consonant system (which has been shown to play the larger role in identifying speech) is relatively uniform and stable.

On a global scale, English is polycentric. There is no one form of English universally accepted as authoritative. Ireland, the USA, Canada and Australia have their own norms, each related to standard written English and to spoken dialectal variation in much the same way as RP. These norms are fully mutually intelligible and acceptable. All are products of the modern period and have undergone no major sound changes. There is increasingly frequent communication among the communities involved. In countries where English is not the native language, the British norm predominates in educational systems in countries which have recently become independent (India, Africa) and more generally in Europe. The General American norm predominates in the Americas and is widely used in the entertainments industry and in industrial management, in which areas it has considerable influence on British usage. Those (e.g. teachers) who have spent a considerable period in one or another English-speaking country are, of course, likely to have learned to conform to its linguistic norms.

At the present time it seems reasonable in a European context to continue (as in the case of Spanish and French) to adhere to the norms of the European rather than the American variety.

At *Waystage*, learners should be able:

- as listeners, to identify the words and expressions used in a slower, but natural colloquial style, by native speakers of the (regionally coloured) standard variants of English (RP, Polite Scottish, Irish, General American and Australian) and by non-native speakers whose speech, though also regionally coloured, approximates to those norms;

- as speakers, to produce spoken English which is readily intelligible both to native speakers and to non-native speakers who approximate to standard norms.

Among the implications of these objectives are:

- learners should be given experience in listening to a variety of norms, and/or regionally coloured speech (including the principal non-native varieties) which approximate to those norms and remain fully intelligible;

- learners should target one of the native norms (which in a European context may well be British RP), but should not be required or expected to approximate to it more closely than is required for full intelligibility, not only to native English speakers, but also to other non-native learners who have reached *Waystage*.

Accordingly, learners at *Waystage* should be aware of the pronunciation in RP of the words and expressions proposed as exponents. That is to say:

- they will be aware of the relation between the sound and spelling of English words, in their vocabulary avoiding simple orthoepic errors;

- they will be aware of and preserve in their own speech the vowel and, particularly, consonant contrasts of the English model they adopt;

- they will be aware of and preserve in their own speech the placement of stress in polysyllabic words;

- they will be able to distinguish by ear non-homophonous English words and expressions;

- they will be aware of some of the principal meaningful contrasts in utterances carried by stress placement and intonation and will be able to recognise and understand them in the speech of others;

- they will be aware of the principal respects in which the accent of learners with their mother tongue background deviates from RP in ways which are likely to impede recognition and thus communication.

Some form of phonetic transcription conforming to the principles of the International Phonetic Association (IPA), e.g. that used in D. Jones: *An English Pronouncing Dictionary*, 14th. edn. ed. A.C. Gimson, or in one of the major monolingual or bilingual dictionaries, may be found useful for raising awareness and for reference purposes, but does not in itself constitute part of the *Waystage* objective.

Intonation

The intonation of English (RP) is described in detail in such works as G.F. Arnold and J.D. O'Connor: *The Intonation of Colloquial English*. It is used by native speakers on the one hand to indicate the informational structure of sentences, and on the other to express nuances of meaning, to indicate unspoken implications or reservations and to convey attitudes and emotional states. As such it plays a very important part in communication and is a frequent source of intercultural misunderstandings. Learners at *Waystage* should recognise and understand the most common intonations used in RP for such purposes. In their own speech they should organise the phrasing, stressing and rhythm of tone groups in accordance with RP norms, and employ rising and falling nuclei appropriately.

Where language forms are cited in this book (e.g. as exponents of language functions or examples of grammatical or lexical entries) the most common intonation pattern (not always the only one possible) is shown in accordance with the conventions shown below. These conventions are similar, but not identical, to those used by Arnold and O'Connor (1961).

A full treatment of English intonation is beyond the scope of this book. The most important features at *Waystage* are tone groups. For the most part, learners at *Waystage* will express themselves in fairly short simple sentences, each consisting of a single tone group. Within the tone group, stressed syllables are spoken in a regular rhythm, unstressed syllables being made to fit in between the beats. The stressed syllables of words which convey lexical information (mainly nouns, adjectives, principal verbs and adverbs) are given prominence in the intonation pattern, unless the information has already been mentioned or is obvious in context. In that case, whilst continuing to mark the rhythmic beat, they are not given pitch prominence. At *Waystage*, two points of pitch prominence are of importance, the *nucleus* and the *head*. The last prominent stressed syllable in a tone group is its *nucleus*, which initiates a pitch pattern which continues to the end of the tone group, including any unstressed or stressed but non-prominent syllables that follow. The pattern used is closely related to the language function of the sentence and its grammatical category. At *Waystage*, five nuclear tones should be distinguished:

1 *Low falling* This is marked in a text by a left to right diagonal falling mark, below the line of writing, placed before the nuclear syllable [ˌ]. This mark is to be interpreted as indicating that the next syllable is stressed. Its vowel starts on a clear level, low-mid tone. The voice then drops to a low creaky note and remains on this low pitch until the end of the tone group.

2 *High falling* This is similar to the low fall, except that the nuclear vowel starts on a pitch above the mid point. It is marked by placing the mark above the line of writing [ˈ].

3 *Low rising* This is marked by a rising mark placed before the nuclear syllable and below the line of writing [ˌ]. It indicates that the next syllable is stressed. Its vowel starts on a clear, low level pitch. There is then a continuous glide upward, but not rising above mid, until the end of the tone group. The glide occurs within the nuclear syllable if it is the last in the group.

It is followed by one or more non-prominent syllables (the 'tail'), stressed or unstressed, the nuclear syllable is spoken on a low level pitch and the rise spans the tail.

4 *High rising* This is shown by placing the rising mark above the line of writing [ˈ]. It indicates that the nuclear vowel starts somewhere between low and mid level, and that the upward glide extends well above mid.

5 *Falling-rising* This may be seen as a sequence of 2 and 3. The nuclear vowel starts high-mid pitch and drops to a low creak. An upward glide follows, which does not go above mid. This tone is indicated by a v-shaped mark placed before the nuclear syllable above the line of writing [˅]. *Waystage* learners should be made aware of the following uses of nuclear tones and be stimulated to use them themselves as appropriate.

1 *Low falling* [ˌ] is used

a) in declarative sentences

   i) for factual statements e.g. identifying, defining, describing and narrating as well as in answers to *wh* questions (which may be short phrases or single words);
   'This is a ˌdoor. They 'drove to ˌLondon. 'Dogs are ˌanimals.

ii) for expressing definite agreement or disagreement, firm denials, firm acceptance or rejection of an offer, definite statements of intention, obligation, granting or withholding permission, etc. In general, it indicates an unambiguous certainty.
That's 'quite ˌright. You 'must ·eat your ˌdinner.

b) in interrogative sentences answerable by *yes* or *no*

i) in tag questions, to invite agreement to a statement that is not in doubt;
'This ·tastes ˌnice, | ˌdoesn't it?

ii) in choice questions, to indicate that the list of options is closed.
'Would you prefer ˌtea | or ˌcoffee?

c) in *wh* questions as a definite request for a piece of information
'Where is the ˌtoilet, ·please?

d) in imperative sentences

i) as a direct order or prohibition;
'Sit ˌdown. 'Don't ˌsmoke in ·here, ·please.

ii) as an instruction;
ˌPush | to 'open the ˌdoor.

iii) as a strong form of offer.
'Have ·one of ˌmy ciga·rettes.

2 *High falling* ['] is used

a) in declarative sentences

i) in exclamations to indicate surprise, protest, enthusiasm, emphasis or insistence;
That's 'excellent! You are 'hurting me! 'Fancy 'that!

ii) to indicate contrast with an element previously mentioned or believed to be in the listener's mind.

'Elbruz is the ·highest ·mountain in ·Europe (not Mont Blanc).

b) in rhetorical questions of an exclamatory type, to which no answer is sought
'Isn't she 'beautiful?

c) in imperative sentences to indicate the urgency of an instruction (e.g. because of imminent danger)
'Stop. 'Don't 'move.

3 *Low rising* [ˌ] is used

   a) in interrogative questions, answerable by *yes* or *no*

      i) to ask politely for confirmation or disconfirmation (also in tag questions);
      You're ˈFrench, | ˌaren't you?

      ii) to make polite requests and offers;
      ˈWould you ·please ·open the ˌwindow? ˈCan I do ·anything to ˌhelp?

      iii) in choice questions, to indicate that the list is open.
      ˈWould you ·like ˌtea | or ˌcoffee | or ˈsomething ˌstronger?

4 *High rising* [ˈ] is used

   a) in declarative sentences (including isolated phrases and words used instead of full sentences)

      i) to convert a statement into a question;
      You were ·born in ˈScotland?

      ii) to query what someone has said.
      You ·say you're ˈthirsty?

   b) (with the *wh* word as nucleus) to ask for repetition of information given but not heard (or understood)
   (He ·lives in (unintelligible).)
   He ·lives ˈwhere? ˈWhere does he ·live?

5 *Falling–rising* [˅] is used

   a) in declarative sentences to convey various implications

      i) warnings;
      That ·jug is ˅hot!

      ii) corrections;
      Her ·dress ˈisn't ˅blue, | it's ˅green.

      iii) implying that something has been left unsaid, which contrasts with, or contradicts what has been overtly stated. ®
      Your o·pinion is ˅interesting. (**implying:** but I ˈdon't ˌagree with it)

   b) in imperative sentences for issuing warnings rather than commands or instructions
   ˈWatch where you're ˅going. ˈDon't ·try to ˅pull the ·door ·open.

Every tone group contains a *nucleus*. Many short utterances will comprise a single tone group, containing only one prominent syllable, which is then the nucleus of the tone group. Where there is more than one prominent syllable, the last of these is the nucleus and the first is the *head*. The head is usually marked by a jump up in pitch to a high-mid level. The actual pitch varies from mid to high, depending on the attitude of the speaker towards what he is saying and towards the hearer. The higher the level, the more cheerful and friendly the speaker sounds. The (high) head is marked in the texts by an upright line before the syllable concerned, above the line of writing [ˈ].

Non-prominent syllables, stressed or unstressed, which precede the head, are spoken on a low-mid pitch. Those following a high head are kept on the same level, or on a descending scale. Those following the nucleus conform to the configuration of the nucleus, as elaborated above. Stressed non-prominent syllables are marked in texts by a dot raised to mid-letter height [·]. As stated, they mark rhythmic beats in the utterance, but have no effect on the pitch pattern. Non-prominent unstressed syllables are left unmarked.

Many, perhaps most, short exchanges in conversation – especially the contributions of learners at *Waystage* – consist of single tone groups. Longer utterances may simply juxtapose tone groups as already described. However, in slower speech sentences contain two or more closely linked tone groups. The boundaries between constituent tone groups are marked [||]. The following are the most common types of sequence, and should be within the productive and receptive competence of *Waystage* learners:

1 Unemphatic, non-constructive sentences
   non-final   final group
   low rising   low falling
   ˈWhen you ·see ˌJohn | ˈtell him to ˌphone me.

2 Contrastive or emphatic
   falling–rising   high falling
   Tomˇorrow | ˈwe are ·going to ˈTurkey.

3 Main statement and modifier
   (non-contrastive)
   low falling   low rising
   I'm ·leaving for ˌGermany | on ˌFriday.

4 Main statement and supplement
   low fall   low fall
   He ˈlives in ˌLondon | in a ˈlarge ·house in ˌPeckham.

Appendix B   Grammatical summary

Introduction

This summary presents a classified inventory of the grammatical categories, elements and structures which figure as exponents of the functional and notional categories set out in Chapters 3–5.

The order of presentation is ascending. That is to say that we first present grammatical information at the word level, classified according to the traditional part of speech with which we expect most users to be familiar. Information is provided concerning the forms of words. Sub-classes are established in terms of the types and functions of words in the major classes set up. Phrases and clauses are then classified according to their formal structure and functional roles in the sentence. Finally, sentences are classified according to their structure and functions. At all points cross reference is made to the relevant sections of Chapters 3, 4 and 5. The same form of reference is used as that employed in the word index, i.e. first the chapter, then the section and sub-sections into which the chapter is divided. So for example, 4.3.2 refers to Chapter 4, section 3.2. Examples are given, using only vocabulary items which figure in the word index.

The summary is not conceived as a teaching or reference grammar of English, but as a guide to the resources to which a learner has access as a result of learning English to *Waystage*.

Many critics of the original *Waystage* appear to have formed the impression that the functional and notional organisation adopted implied a neglect of grammar. We trust that a representation of grammatical content in a more systematic form than that originally adopted (which alphabetised the presentation for ease of reference) may correct that impression. In fact, the grammatical content is very rich and a learner who was able to exploit fully the resources required for the realisation of the range of functions and, particularly, general notions set out in Chapters 3 and 4 would have progressed well beyond what is to be expected from one year's part-time study. In a one-year media-led part-time course, we may expect learners to have encountered the categories, elements and structures listed and to recognise and understand them within the limits of the available vocabulary. Productive capacity is likely to be more restricted, treating many sentences as formulaic, or as a fixed frame within which limited lexical substitutions are made. Much use may be made of words and phrases as short questions and answers in conversation with a co-operative partner. It will, however, be seen that effective use of the simple means presented here provides a surprisingly wide communicative range.

We trust that with a little experience users will find that the systematic presentation enables reference to be made quickly and efficiently as a further aid to curricular planning and course construction.

A   Word level

A 1   Nouns

1.1   Types of noun

1.1.1   proper (with initial capital letter)

1.1.1.1   names of persons
'This is ·John ˌSmith.

1.1.1.2   places
We ·live in ˌSheffield.

1.1.1.3   days (4.3.2)
To 'day is ·Friday the ˌ13th.

1.1.1.4   months (4.3.2)
Our 'holiday is in ˌAugust.

1.1.1.5   festivals (4.3.3)
ˌChristmas is ·coming.

1.1.1.6   religion (5.1.13)
Our 'friends are ˌBaptists.

1.1.2   common

1.1.2.1   uncountable

1.1.2.1.1   abstract
arts, sports, games (5.4.2)
I ·like 'music and ˌsport.
cardinal numbers (4.4.1)
'Three and ˌsix | make ˌnine.
colours (4.5.1.8)
'Are ·black and ·white ˌcolours?

points of compass (4.2.1)
Go 'ten ·miles ˌnorth, | 'then ˌeast.
weather (5.13.1)
We'll have ˋfog | to ˌnight.

1.1.2.1.2   material and mass substances
drinks (5.9.1)
'Have some more ˌwine!
foodstuffs (5.9.1)
A'nother ·slice of 'toast?
meals (5.3.1, 5.9.1)
'When is ˌlunch?
means of transport (5.5.1, 5.5.2)   'Let's ·go by ˌbicycle!
fluids (5.9.1, 5.10.8)
'Where can I ·get ˌwater?
collectives
traffic (5.5.3)
The 'traffic was ˌlight.
police (5.10.5)
The po·lice were 'very ˌhelpful.
underwear (5.8.3)
I 'want to ·wash my ˌunderwear.

1.1.2.1.3   verbal nouns (gerund)
I ˋhate ˌshopping.

1.1.2.2   countables
individuals belonging to classes of
persons
·Nurses ·work 'very ˌhard.
things
I'd ·like a ˌsandwich.

events
He has ·had an ˌaccident.
measures
It is 'two ·miles ˌlong.

1.2 Forms

1.2.1 singular
uninflected form of noun
egg, potato, wife, child

1.2.2 plural

1.2.2.1 regular N+(e)s
eggs, potatoes

1.2.2.2 irregular

1.2.2.2.1 with modified stem
wife   wives (5.1.12)
knife   knives (5.8.4)

1.2.2.2.2 other irregular formations
child   children (5.1.12)
foot   feet (5.7.1)
man   men (5.1.6)
tooth   teeth (5.7.1)
woman   women (5.1.6)
fish   fish (5.9.1)

1.2.2.3 nouns found in the plural only
clothes (5.8.3), people (4.8.2),
tights (5.8.3), trousers (5.8.3)

1.2.2.4 uncountables

1.2.2.4.1 in the sense of 'kinds of'
'Most ·German ·wines are
ˌwhite.

1.2.2.4.2 'objects made of …' nylons,
papers, plastics

1.2.2.4.3 'servings of'
'Two ˌteas and 'three
ˌcoffees, ·please.

1.2.3 possessives (persons and
animals only) (4.7.5.1)

1.2.3.1 singular
N+'s
my 'aunt's ˌdog

1.2.3.2 plural (not ending in s) 's
the 'men's ˌbosses
(ending in s)' only
the 'wives' ˌclub

A2 Pronouns

2.1 demonstrative (3.1.1, 4.8.1.1,
4.8.1.2)
this, that, these, those

2.2 personal (3.1.1, 4.8.1.1,
4.8.1.2)

2.2.1 subject forms
I, you, he, she, it, we, they

2.2.2 non-subject forms
me, you, him, her, it, us, them

2.3 possessive (4.7.5.1, 4.8.1.1,
4.8.1.2)
mine, yours, his, hers, ours,
theirs

2.4 relative ® (4.8.1.2)
who, which, that

2.5 interrogative (4.8.1.1)
who, what, which

2.6 indefinite (4.8.2)
someone ®, (not) … anyone,
nobody ®, something, not …
anything, nothing, everything,
all, some, it

2.7 propword (4.8.1.2)
one

A3 Determiners

3.1 definite article (3.1.1, 4.8.1.1,
4.8.1.2)
the

3.2 indefinite article (4.8.2)

3.2.1 before consonant
a

3.2.2   before vowel
an

3.3   demonstrative (3.1.1, 4.2.1,
4.8.1.1, 4.8.1.2)
this, that, these, those

3.4   possessive (4.7.5.1, 4.8.1.1,
4.8.1.2)
my, your, his, her, its, our, their

3.5   quantitative (4.4)

3.5.1   indefinite (4.4.2)
some, (not) any, no, all, a lot of,
enough, much ℝ, many, more,
most, (a) few, (a) little

3.5.2   cardinal numerals (4.4.1)
one, two, three, etc.

3.5.3   additive (4.4.1)
another

3.6   relative ℝ (4.8.1.2)
which, what, whose

3.7   interrogative (4.8.1.1)
whose, what, which

3.8   distributive (4.4.1)
another

A4   Adjectives

4.1   degree (4.4.3)

4.1.1   equality and inequality
(4.7.4.1)
same, different, another, like,
such ℝ

4.1.2   comparative degree
regular forms (4.4.3, 4.7.4.2)

4.1.2.1   (monosyllabic adjs) adj+er
a 'smaller ˌchild

4.1.2.2   (disyllabic adjs in -y) -y>-i+er
an 'easier ˌquestion

4.1.2.3   (polysyllabic) more + adj
a ˌmore 'careful ˌdriver

4.1.3   superlative degree, regular
forms (4.4.3)

4.1.3.1   (monosyllabic adjs) adj+est
the 'loudest ˌmusic

4.1.3.2   (disyllabic adjs in -y) y>i+est
my 'happiest ˌday

4.1.3.3   (polysyllabics) most + adj
the ˌmost ex'pensive ˌrestaurant

4.1.4   irregular comparatives and
superlatives
good, better, best
bad, worse, worst
much, more, most
little, less, least

4.1.5   ordinal numbers (4.4.1)
first, second, third, etc.

4.2   complementising adjectives

4.2.1   certainty (3.2.9)
sure, certain ℝ
I am 'sure he will ˌcome. ℝ

A5   Adverbs

5.1   Types and functions

5.1.1   of time (3.1.5.(b), 4.3)
now, then, soon, … ago, today,
tomorrow, yesterday, tonight;
early, late;
before, already, yet;
afterwards, later (on); first …
then;
just; always, never, (not) often,
once ℝ, sometimes, twice ℝ,
usually, daily ℝ, weekly ℝ,
monthly ℝ; again, suddenly

5.1.2   existential (4.1)
there, here, away

5.1.3   of place (4.2):
here, there, nowhere ℝ,
everywhere, somewhere,
(not) anywhere, inside, outside,
near, far, away

5.1.4 of direction (4.2.5)
away, back, down, in, out, left,
right, straight (on), up
east, north, south, west

5.1.5 of degree (4.4.3)
enough, too ..., very ..., a little,
a lot, much, almost, quite ®,
rather ®, only, (4.7.6.9)
(See also below.)

5.1.6 of quality (4.5.2.2)
(not) (very) well

5.1.7 of manner (4.7.3.8)
badly, fast, hard, quickly,
slowly, well, adjective+ly

5.1.8 of conjunction (4.7.6.1)
also ®, too, together

5.1.9 of effect (4.7.6.5)
then ..., so ...

5.1.10 indefinite (4.8.2)
everywhere, (not) ... anywhere,
somewhere, nowhere ®,
sometimes, never, always

5.1.11 interrogative (3.1.4, 3.6.3)
how? (4.7.3.8), when? (4.3.3),
where? (4.2.1), why? (4.7.6.4)

5.2 **Form of adverbs**

5.2.1 simple e.g. fast, hard, then

5.2.2 adjective+ly e.g. slowly, badly
carefully, certainly

5.2.3 comparative and superlative
grades of adverbs (gradable
adverbs only)

5.2.3.1 regular

5.2.3.1.1 (monosyllabic)
faster, harder, fastest, hardest

5.2.3.1.2 (disyllabic in -y, not adj+ly)
y>i+er
earlier, earliest

5.2.3.1.3 (polysyllabic, including
adj+ly)

more, most + adv
e.g. more slowly, most quickly

5.2.3.2 irregular
well, better, best
badly, worse, worst
much, more, most
little, less, least

....

A6   Prepositions

6.1 of position (4.2.2)
against ®, among ®, at,
behind, between, in, on,
opposite ®, under, with

6.2 of direction (4.2.5)
across ®, down ®, from, into,
past, through, to, up ®

6.3 of origin (4.2.5, 5.1.9)
from

6.4 of arrangement (4.2.7)
after, before, between

6.5 of time (4.3.3, 4.3.4, 4.3.26)
at, in, on; before, after;
during ®, for, since, till,
until ®, to

6.6 of quantity (4.4.1)
about

6.7 of agency (4.7.3.1, 4.7.3.2)
by

6.8 of giving (4.7.3.3)
to

6.9 of instrumentality (4.7.3.4)
with, by (4.5.1)

6.10 of benefit (4.7.3.5)
for

6.11 of possession (4.7.5.1)
of, with, without

6.12 of focusing (4.7.6.9)
about

A7   Verbs

7.1   Simple form

7.1.1   be

7.1.1.1 simple present, affirmative
(I) am; (you, we, they) are;
(he, she, it) is

7.1.1.2 simple present, negative
(I) am not/I'm not;
(you, we, they) are not/aren't;
(he, she, it) is not/isn't

7.1.1.3 simple present, interrogative
am/aren't (I)?
are/aren't (you, we, they)?
is/isn't (he, she, it)?

7.1.1.4 simple past, affirmative
(I, he, she, it) was;
(you, we, they) were

7.1.1.5 simple past, negative
(I, he, she, it) wasn't;
(you, we, they) weren't

7.1.1.6 simple past, interrogative
was/wasn't (I, he, she, it)?
were/weren't (you, we, they)?

7.1.1.7 verb stem, infinitive and
imperative be

7.1.1.8 present participle and gerund
being

7.1.1.9 past participle been

7.1.2   have

7.1.2.1 simple present, affirmative
(I, you, we, they) have;
(he, she, it) has

7.1.2.2 simple present, negative
(I, you, we, they) haven't;
(he, she, it) hasn't

7.1.2.3 simple present, interrogative
have/haven't (I, you, we, they)?
has/hasn't (he, she, it)?

7.1.2.4 simple past, affirmative
(all persons) had

7.1.2.5 simple past, negative
(all persons) had not/hadn't

7.1.2.6 simple past, interrogative
had/hadn't (all persons)?

7.1.2.7 verb stem, infinitive and
imperative have

7.1.2.8 present participle and gerund
having

7.1.2.9 past participle had

7.1.3   do

7.1.3.1 simple present, affirmative
(I, you, we, they) do;
(he, she, it) does

7.1.3.2 simple present, negative
(I, you, we, they) do not/don't;
(he, she, it) does not/doesn't

7.1.3.3 simple present, interrogative
don't (I, you, we, they)?
doesn't (he, she, it)?

7.1.3.4 simple past, affirmative
(all persons) did

7.1.3.5 simple past, negative
(all persons) did not/didn't

7.1.3.6 simple past, interrogative
did/didn't (all persons)?

7.1.3.7 verb stem, infinitive and
imperative do

7.1.3.8 present participle and gerund
doing

7.1.3.9 past participle done

7.1.4   modal auxiliaries (no non-
finite forms or compound
tenses; no differentiation
according to person)

7.1.4.1 can

7.1.4.1.1 present, affirmative can

7.1.4.1.2 present, negative
cannot/can't

7.1.4.1.3 present, interrogative
can/can't?

7.1.4.1.4 past, affirmative could

7.1.4.1.5 past, negative
could not/couldn't

7.1.4.1.6 past, interrogative
could/couldn't?

7.1.4.2 may

7.1.4.2.1 present, affirmative may

7.1.4.2.2 present, negative may not

7.1.4.2.3 present, interrogative
(affirmative) may?

7.1.4.2.4 present interrogative
(negative) mayn't? ❻

7.1.4.3 must

7.1.4.3.1 present, affirmative must

7.1.4.3.2 present, negative
must not/mustn't

7.1.4.4 shall

7.1.4.4.1 present, interrogative
(affirmative) shall? ❻

7.1.4.4.2 simple past affirmative
should ❻

7.1.4.5 will

7.1.4.5.1 present, affirmative will/'ll

7.1.4.5.2 present, negative
will not/won't

7.1.4.5.3 present, interrogative
(affirmative) will?

7.1.4.5.4 present, interrogative
(negative) won't?

7.1.4.5.5 past, affirmative would/'d

7.1.4.5.6 past, negative
would not/wouldn't/'d not

7.1.4.5.7 past, interrogative
(affirmative) would?

7.1.4.5.8 past, interrogative
(negative) wouldn't?

7.1.5 other verbs, regular

7.1.5.1 simple present, affirmative

7.1.5.1.1 (I, you, we they) verb stem
They ˌask.

7.1.5.1.2 (he, she, it, NP) verb stem+s
He arˌrives.

7.1.5.1.3 verb stem+es
He ˌteaches.

7.1.5.1.4 verb stem
(replacing -y by -i) +es
He ˌtries.

7.1.5.2 simple present, negative

7.1.5.2.1 (I, you, we, they) do
not/don't + infinitive
I 'don't ˌask.

7.1.5.2.2 (he, she, it, NP) does
not/doesn't + infinitive
She 'doesn't ˌtry.

7.1.5.3 simple present, interrogative
(affirmative)

7.1.5.3.1 do (I, you, we, they)
+ infinitive?
'Do you ˌsmoke?

7.1.5.3.2 does (he, she, it, NP)
+ infinitive?
'Does he ˌdance?

7.1.5.4 simple present, interrogative
(negative)

7.1.5.4.1 don't (I, you, we, they)
+ infinitive?
'Don't you ˌsmoke?

7.1.5.4.2 doesn't (he, she, it, NP)
+ infinitive?
'Doesn't it ˌmatter?

7.1.5.5 simple past, affirmative (all
persons)

7.1.5.5.1 verb stem+d
He ar,rived.

7.1.5.5.2 verb stem+ed
I ,asked.

7.1.5.5.3 verb stem (replacing -y by -i) +ed
She ,tried.

7.1.5.6 simple past, negative (all persons)

7.1.5.6.1 did not/didn't + infinitive
They 'didn't ,mind.

7.1.5.7 simple past, interrogative (affirmative, all persons)

7.1.5.7.1 did + NP + infinitive?
'Did you ,like it?

7.1.5.8 simple past, interrogative (negative, all persons)

7.1.5.8.1 didn't + NP + infinitive?
'Didn't they ,play?

7.1.5.9 infinitive and imperative

7.1.5.9.1 verb stem
'Listen!

7.1.5.10 present participle and gerund

7.1.5.10.1 verb stem+ing
listening

7.1.5.11 past participle: as simple past, affirmative
listened

7.1.6   Irregular verbs differ from regular verbs only in the simple past, affirmative and the past participle. The following table shows a) the verb stem (infinitive), b) the simple past, affirmative and c) the past participle for all verbs which figure as exponents of the functional and notional categories listed in Chapters 3, 4 and 5 above.

a)	b)	c)	a)	b)	c)
become	became	become	lose	lost	lost
begin	began	begun	make	made	made
break	broke	broken	put	put	put
bring	brought	brought	read	read	read
buy	bought	bought	say	said	said
come	came	come	see	saw	seen
cut	cut	cut	sell	sold	sold
drink	drank	drunk	send	sent	sent
drive	drove	driven	sing	sang	sung
eat	ate	eaten	show	showed	shown
fall	fell	fallen	sit	sat	sat
feel	felt	felt	sleep	slept	slept
forbid	forbade	forbidden	speak	spoke	spoken
get	got	got	stand	stood	stood
give	gave	given	steal	stole	stolen
go	went	gone	take	took	taken
hear	heard	heard	teach	taught	taught
hurt	hurt	hurt	tell	told	told
keep	kept	kept	think	thought	thought
know	knew	known	understand	understood	understood
leave	left	left	wake	woke	woken
let	let	let	win	won	won
lie	lay	lain	write	wrote	written

7.1.7 compound tenses (all verbs, except modal auxiliaries)

7.1.7.1 present perfect
simple present of have + past participle

7.1.7.2 present continuous
simple past of be + present participle

7.1.7.3 past continuous
simple past of be + present participle ®

7.1.7.4 future/intention
be + going to + infinitive

7.1.7.5 modal auxiliary + infinitive

7.1.7.6 passive voice
be + past participle ®

7.2 **Types of verb**

7.2.1 intransitive verbs, denoting

7.2.1.1 agreement (3.2.1, 3.2.2)
I a͵gree/'don't a͵gree.

7.2.1.2 motion (4.2.4)
We 'sent the ·letter to ͵London.

7.2.1.3 direction (4.2.5)
'Bring the ·book ͵here, ·please.

7.2.1.4 commencement (4.3.24)
The ·programme has ͵started.

7.2.1.5 cessation (4.3.25)
The ͵film has al'ready ͵ended.

7.2.1.6 change, transition (4.3.27)
She has become a ˋmother.

7.2.1.7 sight (4.5.1.4)
'Don't ·look ˇyet!

7.2.1.8 hearing (4.5.1.5)
'Please ͵listen to me.

7.2.1.9 physical condition (4.5.1.10)
My 'father's ͵mother has ·died.

7.2.1.10 accessibility (4.5.1.11)
The ·pub ·closes at '11p͵m. ®

7.2.1.11 expression (4.6.2, 5.12.1)
'Let's ͵talk.

7.2.1.12 address (5.1.2)
I ·live in ͵London.

7.2.1.13 occupation (5.1.10)
I ·work in a ͵hospital.

7.2.1.14 activities of daily life (5.3)
We ·get up ·rather ͵early.

7.2.1.15 leisure activities (5.4)
I 'can't ͵sing ·very ·well.

7.2.1.16 intellectual pursuits (5.4.5)
I 'have to ͵study | and ͵read.

7.2.1.17 sports (5.4.6)
We ˋnever ͵win.

7.2.1.18 weather (5.13.1)
It is ͵raining a·gain.

7.2.2 transitive verbs, denoting

7.2.2.1 factual knowledge (3.2.6)
'Do you ·know my ͵sister?

7.2.2.2 liking (3.2.21)
I ˋlove ͵tennis.

7.2.2.3 moving things (4.2.5)
'Bring me some ͵food ·please.

7.2.2.4 perception (4.5.1.4–6)
'Can you ͵hear me?

7.2.2.5 physical state (4.5.1.3, 4.5.1.10, 5.7.4)
I have 'cut my ͵hand.

7.2.2.6 expression (4.6.2, 5.6.2)
'Write her a ͵letter.

7.2.2.7 possession (4.7.5.1)
'Give him a ͵cheque.

7.2.2.8 activities of daily life (5.3)
We have ·dinner at '8p͵m.

7.2.2.9 leisure activities (5.4)
'Why are you ·watching ·T·V ͵now?

7.2.2.10 sports (5.4.6)
'Do you ·play ͵football?

7.2.2.11 shopping (5.8)
I have ·bought a 'new ˌraincoat.

7.2.2.12 food and drink (5.9)
I 'don't ˌeat | ˌfish.

7.2.2.13 services (5.10)
'Can you ·check the ˌoil, ·please?

7.2.2.14 language (5.12)
'Do you ·speak ˌEnglish?

7.2.3   complementising verbs (for syntax see below) denoting

7.2.3.1 reporting (3.1.2)
He ·says he is ˌhungry.

7.2.3.2 agreement (3.2.3)
I 'don't ·think he is ˅French.

7.2.3.3 knowledge (3.2.5, 3.2.6, 4.6.1), certainty (3.2.9, 3.2.10)
I 'know he ·likes ˌcheese.

7.2.3.4 hope (3.2.24)
I 'hope she will ·come ˅soon.

7.2.3.5 regret (3.2.34)
I am ˌsorry | if you ˌlost.

7.2.3.6 indifference (3.2.35)
I 'don't ˌmind if it ·rains.

7.2.3.7 want, desire (3.2.16, 3.2.17, 3.2.23)
'Do you ·want to ·go ˌhome?

7.2.3.8 requests (3.3.2)
'Do you ·mind ·closing the ˌdoor?

7.2.3.9 expressions (4.6.2)
'Tell him to ·come downˌstairs.

7.3   Usage of verbs

7.3.1   be

7.3.1.1 identifying (3.1.1)
'This is my ˌbicycle.

7.3.1.2 describing (3.1.2)
My ·flat is 'very ˌsmall.

7.3.1.3 correcting (3.1.3)
ˌNo, | she 'isn't ˌFrench, | she is Iˌtalian.

7.3.1.4 asking for confirmation (3.1.4a)
'Are you ˌready?

7.3.1.5 answering for confirmation (3.1.5a)
ˌYes, | I ˌam.

7.3.1.6 location (4.2.1)
I have 'never ˅been | to ˌChina.

7.3.1.7 with predicative adjectives
I am ˌcertain.
This is ˅nice.

7.3.1.8 intention and future reference
be + going to + VP infinitive (4.3.11)
It is ·going to ˅snow.

7.3.1.9 present continuous
be + present participle (4.3.12)
They are ·having ˌdinner.

7.3.1.10 past continuous
past of be + present participle (4.3.13)
He was ·playing ˌchess.

7.3.1.11 age (4.5.1.9)
He is 'twentyˌ-one.

7.3.1.12 price (4.5.2.1)
The ·shoes are £'60.ˌ50.

7.3.1.13 passive voice (4.7.3.2) ®
be + past participle
His ˌglasses have been ·broken. ®

7.3.1.14 origin (5.1.9)
He is from ˌGermany.

7.3.1.15 occupation (5.1.10)
He is a ˌteacher.

7.3.1.16 religion (5.1.13)
They are ˌAnglican.

7.3.1.17 health (5.7.4)
His ·mother is 'very ˌill.

7.3.2 have

7.3.2.1 obligation (3.2.11, 3.2.12)
have + to + VP infinitive
We 'have to `go | ,now.

7.3.2.2 wants, desires (3.2.16, 3.2.17)
'May I ·have a ,drink?

7.3.2.3 availability (4.1.3)
We 'haven't got ·any ,ice.

7.3.2.4 present perfect (4.3.7, 4.3.12, 4.3.18)
have + past participle
'Have you ·seen the ,cat?

7.3.2.5 ownership (4.7.5.1)
have (+ got)
'Have you ·got a ·C,D ·player ·yet?

7.3.2.6 meals (5.3.1)
We have ·lunch at '1 p,m.

7.3.2.7 ailments (5.7.4)
I ·have a 'bad ,cold.

7.3.3 do

7.3.3.1 interrogative (3.1.4)
'Did you ·bring some ,money?

7.3.3.2 tag questions
You `saw them, | ,didn't you?

7.3.3.3 tag responses (3.1.5, 3.2.1)
('Did you ,see him?) `Yes, | I ,did.

7.3.3.4 agreement (3.2.1)
(He ·works `hard.) `Yes, | he `does.

7.3.3.5 negative sentences
It 'doesn't ,matter.

7.3.3.6 denying (3.2.4)
(You ,stole it.) `No, | I `didn't.

7.3.3.7 negative imperatives (3.2.15, 3.3.8)
'Please don't ·smoke ,here.

7.3.3.8 strong hopes (3.2.24)
I `do ·hope | they ,come. ®

7.3.3.9 on being introduced (3.4.6)
'How do you ,do!

7.3.3.10 anaphoric use (4.8.1.2)
He 'asked me to ,stop, | so I ,did.

7.3.3.11 semi-deictic (4.8.2)
'What can we ·do ,now?

7.3.4 can

7.3.4.1 short questions (3.1.4a)
,Can you?

7.3.4.2 short answers
,Yes, I ,can.

7.3.4.3 ability (3.2.7)
I 'can't ,swim.

7.3.4.4 denying possibility (3.2.9e)
He `can't | be ·60 ·years ,old.

7.3.4.5 permission (3.2.13–15)
'Can I go ,out this ·evening?

7.3.4.6 declining an invitation (3.3.5)
I am a·fraid I 'can't ,come. ®

7.3.4.7 offering assistance (3.3.9)
'Can I ,help ·you?

7.3.4.8 requesting assistance (3.3.10)
'Can you ·tell me the ·way to the ,station?

7.3.4.9 sensory perception (4.5.1.4, 4.5.1.5) I can ·see an `island.

7.3.4.10 capacity (4.5.2.7)
·Animals 'cannot ,speak.

7.3.4.11 travel (5.5.1)
'How can I ·get to ,Croydon?

7.3.5 could

7.3.5.1 suggestions (3.3.1)
We could 'drink ˅water. ®

7.3.5.2 requests (3.3.2)
'Could you ·please ,write your ·name? ®

7.3.6 may

7.3.6.1 permission (3.2.13, 3.2.14)
'May I ,smoke? ,Yes, | you ,may.

7.3.7   must

7.3.7.1 with holding permission, forbidding (3.2.15)
You must 'not ·drive too ˌfast.

7.3.8   shall

7.3.8.1 suggestions (3.3.1)
'Shall we ˌeat ·now?

7.3.9   should

7.3.9.1 advice (3.3.7)
You should ·see a ˌdoctor.

7.3.10 will

7.3.10.1 intention (3.2.18, 3.2.19)
I'll 'wash up ˌafterwards. ®

7.3.10.2 requests (3.3.2)
'Will you ·turn off the ˌlights, ·please? ®

7.3.10.3 accepting (3.3.4)
ˌThank you, that will be 'very ˌnice.

7.3.10.4 future reference (4.3.11, 4.3.15)
The 'train will be deˌlayed. ®

7.3.11 would

7.3.11.1 wants, desires (3.2.16, 3.2.17)
'Would you ·like an ·ice,-cream?

7.3.11.2 preference (3.2.20)
I'd pre'fer ˌcoffee.

7.3.11.3 inviting (3.3.3)
'Would you ·like to ·come for ˌlunch?

7.4   Use of verb forms

7.4.1   simple present

7.4.1.1 general statements without time reference (4.3.14)
He ˋnever | ·answers ˌletters.

7.4.1.2 permanent states (4.3.20)
She ·lives in ˌParis.

7.4.1.3 habitual actions (4.3.17)
I 'usually ˌdrive to ·work.

7.4.1.4 present reference with verbs denoting

7.4.1.4.1 cognitive attitudes (3.2.1)
I aˌgree.

7.4.1.4.2 reflection (3.2.9c, 4.6.1)
I be'lieve he'll ˌcome.

7.4.1.4.3 volition (3.2.16–20)
I 'want an ·ice-ˌcream.

7.4.1.4.4 emotions (3.2.21–29)
I 'like ˌswimming.

7.4.2   simple past

7.4.2.1 narrating actions completed in a past period (4.3.13)
We 'went there ˌyesterday.

7.4.2.2 reporting a statement made in the past containing a simple present verb (3.1.2)
I ·said I ·wanted ˋfish.

7.4.2.3 for the equivalents of simple present usage (see above), but relating to a past period

7.4.2.3.1 habitual actions (4.3.17)
I 'went to ˌchurch | 'every ˌSunday.

7.4.2.3.2 cognitive attitudes (3.2.1–15)
I 'knew he was ˌright.

7.4.2.3.3 volition (3.2.16–20)
·Mozart pre·ferred Viˋenna | to ˌSalzburg.

7.4.2.3.4 emotions (3.2.21–29)
I ˋhated ·sports | at ˌschool.

7.4.3   present perfect (with reference to present time)

7.4.3.1 anteriority (4.3.7)
'Have they ˌleft yet?

7.4.3.2 past action leading to a present condition (4.3.12)
The ·soup has ˌburnt.

7.4.3.3 continuity, i.e. present action or state beginning in the past (4.3.18)
I have ·waited ·here for 'two ˛hours.

7.4.4 present continuous

7.4.4.1 action in progress at time of speaking (4.3.12, 4.3.18)
It is ˋsnowing.

7.4.4.2 temporariness (4.3.21)
I am ·feeling ˛ill | this ˛morning.

7.4.4.3 proximal future (4.3.11)
be + going to + VP infinitive
'When is the ·play ·going to ˛start?

7.4.4 past continuous ®

7.4.4.1 reporting actions in progress at a point in the past (4.3.13)
It was ˛raining, | so I 'put my ˛raincoat ·on.

7.4.5 passive voice ®

7.4.5.1 objective as subject (4.7.3.2)
This ·door must 'not be ˛closed.

A8   Conjunctions

8.1   Co-ordinating

8.1.1 conjunctive

8.1.1.1 non-contrastive **and** (4.7.6.1)
'Mary and ˛Jane | are ˛friends.

8.1.1.2 contrastive **but** (4.7.6.1)
Those ·shoes are ˇgood, | but ex˛pensive.

8.1.2 disjunctive **or** (4.7.6.2)
'Do you want ˛coffee | or ˛tea?

8.2   Subordinating

8.2.1 complementising **that** ®
I 'hope that he will ˛come. ®

8.2.2 adverbial

8.2.2.1 time **when** (3.1.4,5, 4.3.3)
(I'll 'leave) when the ˛doctor ar·rives.

8.2.2.2 place **where** (3.1.4,5, 4.2.1)
'Please ·tell me ·where you ˛live.

8.2.2.3 reason, cause **because** (4.7.6.4)
(I 'work) be·cause I ˛have to.

8.2.2.4 condition **if** (4.7.6.8)
ˋI don't ·mind | if you ˛smoke.

B   Phrase level

B1   Noun phrase (NP)

1.1 pronoun (4.8.1) I like it.

1.2 noun without determiner

1.2.1 proper names
'Jean-˛Paul | ·lives in ˛Paris.

1.2.2 plural indefinites
'Animals ·eat ˛plants.

1.2.3 unspecified singular names denoting

1.2.4 colour (4.5.1.8)
'Blue is a ˛cold ·colour.

1.2.5 material (4.5.1.13)
'Is this ·skirt ·made of ˛wool?

1.2.6 days, months (4.3.3, 5.1.4)
To'day is ˛Monday.

1.2.7 drinks (5.9.1)
I 'don't ˋdrink | ˛beer.

1.2.8 foodstuffs (5.9.1)
'Ice-˛cream | is 'very ˛nice.

1.2.9 meals (5.3.1, 5.9.1)
'Dinner is at ·8 p˛m.

1.2.10 festivals (4.3.3)
'Will you ·stay at ˛home for ·Christmas?

1.2.11 numerals (4.4.1)
'Two and ˏtwo | make ˎfour.

1.2.12 languages (3.6.9)
She ·speaks 'English, ·French and ˎGerman.

1.2.13 arts, sports and games (5.4.2, 5.4.6)
He 'plays ˇfootball, | but 'also ·listens to ˎmusic.

1.2.14 means of transport (5.5.1, 5.5.2)
We 'travelled to ˏPortugal | by ˎtrain.

1.3 determiner + noun (cf A3 above)
'Some ·people ·like a ˎdog in their ·house.

1.4 (determiner +) adjective + noun
I 'like a ·good ˎfilm.

1.5 (determiner +) qualifying adverb + adjective + noun
His ·wife is a 'very ·nice ˎwoman.

1.6 (determiner+) (adjective+) noun denoting container (4.4.2)
I'd like a 'nice ·cup of ˎtea.
or measure (4.2.2, 4.2.8.4, 4.2.8.5)+ of + mass nouns or plural NP
A 'pound of ˎapples, ·please.

B2 Use of noun phrase

2.1 as subject (4.7.3.1)
My 'new ˏdentist | is 'very ˎgood.

2.2 as direct object of a transitional verb (4.7.3.2)
I ˋhate | ·cold ˏcoffee.

2.3 as indirect object of a verb of giving (4.7.3.3)
'Give your ·father a ·new ˎtie.

2.4 in prepositional phrases
He ·works in a 'very ·large ˎhospital.

B3 Pronoun phrase (Pron. P)

3.1 demonstrative + one (3.1.1)
I'd 'like ˎthat one, ·please.

3.2 determiner + adjective + one (4.8.1.2)
'Give me a ˎbigger one, ·please.

3.3 indefinite pronoun of quantity (4.4.2, 4.8.2) + of + NP
'Some of these ˏapples are ˎbad.

B4 Verb phrase (VP)

4.1 phrases containing one main verb (for forms and uses see A above)

4.1.1 intransitive verb
'What ˎhappened?

4.1.2 copula + complement (NP or AdjP)
The ·man is 'very ˎill.

4.1.3 transitive verb + direct object (NP)
They ·eat ˎvegetables.

4.1.4 transitive verb + indirect object + direct object
'Give me the ˎletter.

4.1.5 adverb + verb
I ˋnever | ˎsmoke.

4.1.6 verb + adverb(s)
'Come ˎhome ·now.

4.1.7 verb + prepositional phrase
We 'drove on the ˎmotorway.

4.1.8 short answers (3.1.5, 3.2) auxiliary or pro-verb

4.1.8.1 be
(Is that enough?) ˎYes, | it ˎis.

4.1.8.2 have
(Have they eaten?) ˎNo, | they ˎhaven't.

4.1.8.3 modals
(Can I go now?) ˎYes, | you ˎcan.

4.1.8.4 do
(Don't you agree?) ˎYes, | I ˎdo.

4.2   Nominalised VPs

4.2.1   to + VP infinitive

4.2.1.1 following verbs expressing wants and desires (3.2.16)
I'd 'like to ·go to the ˎtheatre.

4.2.2   VP gerund

4.2.2.1 following verbs expressing dislike (3.2.22) ®
I 'hate ·saying goodˎbye. ®

4.2.2.2 in suggestions and invitations (3.3.1, 3.3.3) ®
'What about ·playing ˎtennis? ®

4.2.2.3 in requests (3.3.2) ®
'Would you ·mind ·sitting ˎdown? ®

B5   Adverb phrase (AdvP)

5.1   adverb of degree + gradable adverb (4.7.3.8)
He ·works 'very ˎhard.

5.2   prepositional phrase
We 'eat in the ˎkitchen.

B6   Preposition phrase (PrepP)

6.1   preposition + NP + of (4.2.2)
The 'bus ·stops in ·front of the ˋbank | at the 'end of the ˎroad.

6.2   next to
'Your ˎbedroom | is 'next to the ˎbathroom.

6.3   far from
The ho·tel is 'not ·far from the ˎstation.

C   Clause level

C1   Clause types and functions

1.1   main clause (NP + VP finite), as

1.1.1   sole constituent of a simple sentence
'Jaap is ˎDutch.

1.1.2   co-ordinate constituent of a compound sentence
'Jaap is ˎDutch | and his 'wife is ˎEnglish.

1.1.3   main clause in a complex sentence
I 'hope it ·won't ˎrain.

1.2   Subordinate clause

1.2.1   as short answer to a wh question
('Why are you ˎwaiting?)
Be·cause my ·friend is ˎlate.

1.2.2   as part of a complex sentence
'I don't ·mind | if you ˎsmoke.

C2   Forms and functions of subordinate clauses

2.1   (that +) NP + VP finite

2.1.1   following certain complementising adjectives

2.1.1.1 sure, certain (3.2.9a) ®
I'm 'sure (that) she's ˎGreek.

2.1.2 following certain complementising verbs

2.1.2.1 **know, think, believe, (3.2.9, 4.6.1), hope (3.2.24)**
I 'hope | (that) you're ‚well.

2.1.2.2 **say, tell + NP (3.1.2, 4.6.2)**
She 'says (that) she's his ‚sister.

2.2 **if + NP + VPfinite**

2.2.1 in indirect questions, following **ask**
He 'asks if he can ‚go ·now.

2.2.2 after **mind**, e.g. asking permission (3.2.14)
'Do you ·mind if we ·go by ‚air?

2.2.3 expressing a condition **wh + NP + VPfinite**
He will 'eat an ·egg if it is ˅boiled.

2.3 adverbial of time **when**
I will 'come when you ‚call.

2.4 adverbial of place **where**
He will 'follow where you ‚go.

2.5 **because + NP + VPfinite**
I 'came be·cause you 'asked me.

3 **pro-clause**

3.1 **so**
(Will it rain?) I ˅think so.

3.2 **not**
(Will it snow?) I ˅hope not.

D   Sentence level

D1   Form

1.1 simple sentences, consisting of one main clause only (cf. C1.1 above)
I 'must ·go ‚home.

1.2 compound sentences, consisting of two or more main clauses, linked by co-ordinating conjunctions
It is 'late | and I 'must ·go 'home.

1.3 complex sentences, consisting of a main clause linked (by a subordinating conjunction) to a subordinate clause
I 'must ·go ‚home | be·cause it is ‚late.

D2   Sentence types

2.1   Declarative

2.1.1 affirmative
I 'have an ap‚pointment | at 'six o'‚clock.

2.1.2 negative

2.1.2.1 NP + be + not/n't + participle (+ …)
The ·heating is 'not ‚working.

2.1.2.2 + AdjP
I'm 'not ·very ‚hungry.

2.1.2.3 + NP
·Anne is 'not my ‚sister.

2.1.2.4 NP + have + not/n't + past participle (+ …)
I 'haven't ‚seen her.

2.1.2.5 + NP
We 'haven't any ‚milk.

2.1.2.6 NP + do + not/n't + VPinfinitive
I 'don't ·know 'anything | a·bout ‚cricket.

2.1.2.7 affirmative form including negative indefinite pronoun or adverb
She 'never | ·eats ‚fish.

2.1.2.8 negative form + indefinite pronoun or adverb
He ·can't 'ever ·eat ·anything with ˌsugar in it.

2.2 Interrogative

2.2.1 decision (yes/no) questions interrogative sentence structure, i.e.

2.2.1.1 be (+ not/n't) +NP + participle (+ ...)
'Are you ˌcoming?

2.2.1.2 + AdjP?
'Isn't ·lunch ·ready ˌyet?

2.2.1.3 + NP?
'Is this the ˌexit?

2.2.1.4 have (not/n't) + NP + past principle (+ ...)
'Has the ·film ˌstarted ·yet?

2.2.1.5 + NP
'Have you an apˌpointment?

2.2.1.6 modal auxiliary (+ not/n't) + NP + VPinfinitive
'Can you ˌhelp me?

2.2.1.7 do (+ not/n't) + NP + VPinfinitive
'Don't you aˌgree?

2.2.1.8 declarative sentence with high-rising intonation
'That was her ˊhusband?

2.2.1.9 affirmative sentence + negative tag question
That ho·tel is exˋpensive, | ˌisn't it?

2.2.1.10 negative sentence + positive tag question
It 'isn't ˋfar, | ˌis it?

2.2.1.11 response tag question (with same polarity as statement of partner)
(I'm tired.) ˊAre you?

2.2.2 special (wh) questions, requiring an answer containing

2.2.2.1 a subject NP (human)
who + VPfinite
'Who is that ˌman?

2.2.2.2 a subject NP (non-human)
what + VPfinite
'What is ˌthat?

2.2.2.3 specification of a subject NP
which + NP + VPfinite
'Which ho·tel is ˌcheapest?

2.2.2.4 an object NP (human)
who + interrogative sentence structure
'Who do you ˌwant?

2.2.2.5 an object NP (non-human)
what + interrogative sentence structure
'What are you ˌdrinking?

2.2.2.6 a specified NP
which + NP + interrogative sentence structure
'Which ˌnewspaper do you ·read?

2.2.2.7 an adverbial of time
when + interrogative sentence structure
'When does the ˌtrain ·leave?

2.2.2.8 an adverbial of place
where + interrogative sentence structure
'Where do they ˌlive?

2.2.2.9 an adverbial of manner
how + interrogative sentence structure
'How can I ·get to Piccaˌdilly?

2.2.2.10 an adverbial of reason or related declarative sentence
why + interrogative sentence structure
'Why ·didn't you ˌtell me?

2.3   Imperative

2.3.1   VP infinitive (+ please)
'Sit ˌdown, ·please.

2.3.2   let's + VP infinitive
'Let's ·listen to some ˌmusic.

....

D3   Functions of sentence types

3.1   Affirmative sentences

3.1.1   identifying (3.1.1)
'This is my ˌraincoat.

3.1.2   reporting (3.1.2)

3.1.3   narrating an event as it occurs
'Jane ·goes ·into the ˌkitchen. She ·breaks 'two ˌeggs | and ·makes an ˌomelette.

3.1.4   narrating an event in the past
He 'got into the ˌcar | and 'drove a ˌway.

3.1.5   describing people or things
ᵛCarmen | has 'brown ˌeyes | and 'long, ·black ˌhair.

3.1.6   answering questions (3.1.5)
(Would you like a bath?)
I'd pre'fer a ˌshower.

3.1.7   making statements regarding

3.1.7.1 agreement (3.2.1)
I aˌgree.

3.1.7.2 knowledge (3.2.5)
I 'know ˌScotland | 'very ˌwell.

3.1.7.3 certainty (3.2.9)
I am 'sure it will ˌsnow to·night.

3.1.7.4 obligation (3.2.11)
We 'have to ˌdo it.

3.1.7.5 ability (3.2.7)
I 'cannot ·drive a ˌcar.

3.1.7.6 permissibility (3.2.13, 3.2.15)
You can 'get up ˌlate | toˌmorrow.

3.1.8   expressing

3.1.8.1 wants and desires (3.2.16)
I'd 'like a·nother ˌblanket.

3.1.8.2 intentions (3.2.18)
I am ·going to ·buy a 'new ˌcar.

3.1.8.3 preference (3.2.20)
I'd 'rather ·drink ˌwater. ®

3.1.8.4 pleasure, happiness (3.2.21)
This ·food is 'very ˌnice.

3.1.8.5 displeasure, unhappiness (3.2.22)
I ·hate 'everything and ˌeverybody | toˌday. ®

3.1.8.6 liking (3.2.21)
·Mr ·Smith is 'very ˌpleasant. ®

3.1.8.7 dislike (3.2.22)
I ˋhate | ˌshopping. ®

3.1.8.8 satisfaction (3.2.25)
This is 'very ˌgood.

3.1.8.9 dissatisfaction (3.2.26)
I 'don't ˌlike ·this.

3.1.8.10 hope (3.2.24)
I 'hope it will be ˌfine to·morrow.

3.1.8.11 gratitude ®
That is 'very ˌkind ·of you. ®

3.1.8.12 regret ®
I am 'very ˌsorry | if I ˌhurt you. ®

3.1.9   giving

3.1.9.1 suggestions ®
We could 'go to the ᵛtheatre. ®

3.1.9.2 advice ®
You should ·go by ˋtaxi. ®

3.2   Negative sentences

3.2.1   correcting a positive statement (3.1.3)
Her ·dress 'isn't ᵛblue.

3.2.2   denying statements (3.2.4)
I have 'never ˌbeen there.

3.2.3 denying knowledge (3.2.5)
I 'don't ˌknow the ·man.

3.2.4 expressing inability (3.2.7)
I 'can't reˌpair the ·engine.

3.2.5 expressing doubt (3.2.9e)
I 'don't ·think ˇall ·birds can ·fly.

3.2.6 denying obligation (3.2.11)
We 'don't ·have to ˌfollow him.

3.2.7 witholding permission,
forbidding (3.2.15) ⓡ
·Guests must 'not ·play ·music
·after ˌmidnight. ⓡ

3.2.8 expressing negative
preferences (3.2.20) ⓡ
I'd 'rather ·not ·watch
ˌtelevision. ⓡ

3.2.9 expressing displeasure, dislike
(3.2.22)
·Smoking is 'not ·very ˌnice.

3.2.10 hoping something will not
happen
I 'hope he ·won't ·go aˇway.
I ˇhope ·not.

3.2.11 expressing indifference
(3.2.35)
It 'doesn't ˌmatter.
forgiveness (3.2.31)
ˋI don't ˌmind.

3.2.12 signalling non-understanding
(3.6.1)
I 'didn't underˌstand that.

3.3 **Decision questions**

3.3.1 asking for confirmation
(3.1.4a)
'Did you ˌwin?

3.3.2 asking about

3.3.2.1 agreement (3.2.3)
'Don't you ·think she's ˌnice?

3.3.2.2 knowledge (3.2.6)
'Do you ·know my ˌhusband?

3.3.2.3 ability (3.2.8)
'Can you ˌsee ·well?

3.3.2.4 certainty (3.2.10) ⓡ
'Are you ˌsure? ⓡ

3.3.2.5 obligation (3.2.12)
'Do we have to ·wash ·up ˌnow?

3.3.3 seeking permission (3.2.14)
'Can I ·go ·now, ·please?

3.3.4 expressing wants, desires
(3.2.16)
'May I have ·something to
ˌdrink?

3.3.5 enquiring about

3.3.5.1 wants, desires (3.2.17)
'Would you ·like some ˌjam?

3.3.5.2 intentions (3.2.19)
'Are you ·going to ·get ˌup
·soon?

3.3.5.3 likes and dislikes (3.2.23)
'Do you ·like ˌcheese?

3.3.6 making suggestions (3.3.1)
'Shall we ˌdance?

3.3.7 making requests (3.3.2, 3.6.2,
3,6.6, 3.6.7, 3.6.10)
'Could you ·close the ˌdoor,
·please?

3.3.8 inviting someone to do
something (3.3.3)
'Would you ·like to ˌplay with us?

3.3.9 offering assistance (3.3.9)
'Can I ˌhelp you?

3.3.10 requesting assistance (3.3.10)
'Can you ˌcarry this ·for me,
·please?

3.4 **Special (wh) questions**

3.4.1 asking for specific
information (3.1.4b)

3.4.1.1 time when?
'When did he ˌleave?

3.4.1.2 place where?
'Where does she ˌlive?

3.4.1.3 manner how?
'How can I ˌdo it?

3.4.1.4 degree how far/much/ long/hot, etc.?
'How much is that ˌdress?

3.4.1.5 reason why?
'Why did you ˌcome?

3.4.2 seeking identification (3.1.4c)

3.4.2.1 person who?
'Who is your ˌboss?

3.4.2.2 possession whose + NP?
'Whose ˌbag is ·this?

3.4.2.3 thing what?
'What is ˌthat ·thing?

3.4.2.4 which + NP?
'Which ·pet is ˌyours?

3.4.2.5 events What happened?

3.4.3 enquiring about wants and desires (3.2.16)

3.4.3.1 What about + NP
'What about a ·glass of ˌbeer?

3.4.3.2 What would you like?

3.4.4.3 What do you want?

3.4.4 suggesting a course of action (3.3.1)
What about + VPgerund ®
'What about ·going to the ˌcinema?

3.4.5 inviting others to do something? (3.3.3)
What about + VPgerund ®
'What about ·coming ˌhome?

3.4.6 advising others to do something (3.3.7)
Why don't you + VP infinitive?
'Why don't you ˌask her?

3.4.7 asking for partial repetition (3.6.3) (with high-rising intonation on wh word)

3.4.7.1 time (Sorry +) when + interrogative structure
ᵛSorry, | 'when did it ·happen?

3.4.7.2 place (Sorry +) where + interrogative structure
'Where did they ·go?

3.4.7.3 manner (Sorry +) how + interrogative structure
'How do you ·get there?

3.4.7.4 degree (Sorry +) how + far, much, etc.
ᵛSorry, 'how ·far is it?

3.4.7.5 reason (Sorry +) why + interrogative structure
'Why did he ·leave?

3.4.7.6 person (Sorry +) who
ᵛSorry, | 'who did you ·say it was?

3.4.8 asking for clarification (3.6.4) (Sorry +) what is + NP
ᵛSorry, | 'what is a ˌdaffodil?

3.5 Imperative sentences

3.5.1 making suggestions (3.3.1) Let's + VPinfinitive
'Let's ·check the ˌtyres.

3.5.2 making requests (3.3.2)
'Please ·open the ˌwindow.
ˌListen, ·please.

3.5.3 giving warnings (3.3.8)

3.5.3.1 Be ᵛcareful!

3.5.3.2 'Look ᵛout!

3.5.3.3 Don't + VPinfinitive
'Don't be ᵛlate.

3.5.3.4 Mind + NP
'Mind that ᵛknife.

Appendix C Word index

front *n*: **4.2.2**
fruit *n*: **5.9.1**
fry *vb*: **5.9.1**
full (of) *adj*: **4.5.1.14, 5.10.8**
furniture *n*: **5.2.2**

G [dʒiː]

gallon *n*: **4.2.8.5**
garage *n*: **5.2.4, 5.10.7**
garden *n*: **5.2.1**
gas *n*: **5.2.3**
German *n*: **5.12.1**
get *vb*: **4.7.5.1, 5.6.2**
get up *vb*: **4.2.4, 5.3.1**
girl *n*: **5.1.6**
give *vb*: **4.7.5.1**
give way *vb*: **5.5.3**
glass *n* and *adj*: **4.4.2, 5.8.4**
glasses *n pl*: **5.7.5**
go *vb*: **4.2.4, 5.3.1, 5.4.2, 5.5.1, 5.8.1**
go out *vb*: **5.4.1**
going to *vb*: **3.2.18, 4.3.11**
gold *n* and *adj*: **4.5.1.13**
good *adj*: **3.2.25, 3.2.32, 3.2.33, 3.4.2, 3.4.9, 3.5.6, 4.5.2.2**
goodbye *excl*: **3.4.9, 3.5.6**
good-looking *adj*: **5.1.15**
gram(me) *n*: **4.2.8.4**
grass *n*: **5.2.6**
great *adj*: **3.2.28, 3.2.34**
green *adj*: **4.5.1.8**
grey *adj*: **4.5.1.8**
grill *vb*: **5.9.1**
grilled *adj*: **5.9.1**
group *n*: **4.7.6.1**
guest *n*: **5.5.5**

H [eiːtʃ]

hair *n*: **5.7.1**
half *pron*: **4.3.1, 4.3.2, 4.4.2**
hallo! *excl*: **3.4.1, 3.4.2, 3.4.3, 3.4.6**
hand *n*: **5.7.1**
happen *vb*: **4.1.4**
hard *adj*: **4.5.1.7**
hard *adv*: **4.7.3.8**
hat *n*: **5.8.3**

hate *vb*: **3.2.22**
have *vb*: **3.2.16, 4.1.3, 4.7.5.1, 5.3.1, 5.9.1**
have got *vb*: **4.7.5.1**
have to *vb*: **3.2.11, 3.2.12**
he *pron*: **3.1.1**
head *n*: **5.7.1**
hear *vb*: **4.5.1.5**
heart *n*: **5.7.1**
heating *n*: **5.2.3**
heavy *adj*: **4.2.8.3, 4.2.8.4**
help *vb*: **5.10.7**
her *pron*: **3.1.1**
here *adv*: **3.3.2, 3.4.8, 4.1.2, 4.2.1, 4.8.1.2**
high *adj*: **4.2.8.1**
hill *n*: **5.2.5**
him *pron*: **3.1.1**
history *n*: **5.12.1**
hobby *n*: **5.4.2**
holiday(s) *n*: **4.3.2, 5.3.2, 5.4.1**
home *adv*: **5.3.1**
hope *vb*: **3.2.24, 4.6.1**
horse *n*: **5.2.6**
hospital *n*: **5.1.10, 5.7.5**
hot *adj*: **3.1.4(b), 4.2.8.7**
hotel *n*: **5.5.5**
hour *n*: **4.3.2, 4.3.16**
house *n*: **5.2.1, 5.5.5**
how *adv*: **3.1.4(b), 3.4.3, 3.4.6, 3.6.3, 3.6.8, 4.5.1.9, 4.7.3.8**
how much *adv*: **4.5.2.1**
how old *adv*: **4.5.1.9**
hungry *adj*: **5.7.2**
hurry *vb*: **4.2.4**
hurt *vb*: **4.5.1.10, 5.7.4**
husband *n*: **5.1.12**

I [aiː]

I *pron*: **3.1.1**
ice *n*: **5.13.1**
ice-cream *n*: **5.9.1**
if *conj*: **4.7.6.8**
ill *adj*: **4.5.1.10, 5.7.4**
important *adj*: **4.5.2.8**
in *adv*: **4.2.5**
in *prep*: **3.6.9, 4.2.2, 4.3.3, 4.3.11**
in front of *prep*: **4.2.2**

T [tiː]

Open lists

N.B. These lists are 'open' in the sense that we do not try to define a vocabulary for all learners in the areas given. The words a learner needs will depend on circumstances, experience and interests. The examples given in the main text are such as to be likely to be of general use, but learners will need to be able to tell others their own nationality, occupation, etc. even if they are not in the list of examples.

Appendix D   Subject index

Index of language functions and notional categories

In the following index, numbers refer to chapters and items or sections. The chapters referred to are 3, 4 and 5. All references beginning with 3 are to language functions, those beginning with 4 are general notions and those beginning with 5 are references to themes or sub-themes.